Kerala Cuisine

By

Lizy M. Mathai

Flavourful and savoury South Indian dishes made easy and less spicy for all without losing its originality

Copyright 2017 © Lizy M. Mathai
All rights reserved

ISBN:
978-0-9695786-1-1 Kerala Cuisine Book
978-0-9695786-2-8 Kerala Cuisine Digital
978-0-9695786-3-5 Kerala Cuisine Electronic

Published by: Lizy M. Mathai
Kelowna, BC
Pictures: Personal photos
Pixabay.com
Printed in Canada

Dedication

To my parents Mr. P.Joseph Mathews & Mariamma Mathews for their love & encouragement

Acknowledgements

Matt M. Mathai
Sharon L. Babu
Thankamma Rajan
Samuel Mathew
Raj & Rachel
Ron & Zarah
Ray Mathai

KERALA CUISINE

Introduction

Though my friends are from a wide variety of social and cultural backgrounds, they all seem to share a common interest - the love for Kerala cooking. Throughout the years, as friends tasted my Kerala dishes, they often would ask for the recipes. So this book has all those recipes and many more. I'm really excited about sharing my expertise with you, regardless of your background and your varying tastes for food, I know you will enjoy the aroma and flavor of Kerala cooking.

You are probably wondering where Kerala is? Well, Kerala my birthplace is a small beautiful province in South India. Rice is the staple food, which will be the base for many of the dishes in this book. Keralites enjoy three full meals a day, along with two yummy snacks. Housewives cook in many different styles to satisfy their family. One would be amazed by this land of spices and coconuts. It would be difficult to say "no" to the savory and exotic dishes served throughout the day, with great variety, taste and colour. No wonder this book is rich in delicious delicacies.

In the art of creative cooking, my mother was my first teacher. Even though I came from a large family of eight siblings, my mother always found time to cook simple, colorful, and delicious meals that amazed us. Once a week, she would have us cook experimental dishes, which, on occasion, would end in catastrophe. So, through cynical criticisms and loud applauses, my cooking career had a good start at home. Also, as a secretary of a YWCA, I was exposed to fancy cooking that gave me the opportunity to add to my growing expertise. Then, upon completing my Masters in Literature with Education Degree, I taught elementary school teachers in Nigeria for almost 7 years.

KERALA CUISINE

There I had more opportunities to develop and experiment with my unique recipes. After migrating to Canada in 1985, I continued my hobby of cooking and developing more recipes, mastering all the techniques that I had learned from this long history of cook training. I wanted to learn more about the western cooking and this desire made me to take a Cooking Diploma from Vancouver Community College. I have been working as a business instructor in public and private colleges in British Columbia. Many of the recipes are handed down by parents and grandparents.

This book has been designed to make cooking fun and tasty to anyone, regardless of background. All recipes are authentic and tested to suite all tastes without losing their originality.

I hope you'll enjoy not by reading but by trying out the savory recipes in Kerala Cuisine of South India.

My Special thanks to my husband Matt Mathai & Sharon L. Babu who encouraged me to do this project.

Lizy M. Mathai
Kelowna, BC
Canada

KERALA CUISINE

Preface

ENGLISH AND INDIAN EQUIVALENTS

ENGLISH	MALAYALAM	HINDI	PUNJABI
Almond	Badham	Badam	Badam
Asafetida	Kayam	Hing	Hing
Atta Flour	Chappathi Podi	Atta	Atta
Bitter gourd	Pavakka	Karela	Karela
Cabbage	Kabbage	Patta Gobi	Patta Gobi
Caraway Seeds	Cake Jeerakum	Pullao Jeera	Kala Jeera
Cardamom	Elakka	Elaichi	Elaichi
Cauliflower	Koliflower	Phoolgobi	Phoolgobi
Chickpeas	Kadala	Chana	Chana
Cinnamon	Karuva Patta	Dalchini	Dalchini
Cloves	Grambu	Lavang	Laung
Coconut	Thenga	Nariyal	Nariyal
Coriander Leaves	Malli ela	Kotmir	Hara Dhania
Cucumber	Vellarika	Kakadi	Kheera
Cumin	Jeerakam	Jeera	Jeera
Curry Leaves	Karivepila	Curry Patta	Curry Patta
Drum Sticks	Murungikka	ShingFali	Shingh Fali
Dry Ginger	Chukku	Sunt	Sunt
Fennel Seed	Perumjeerakam	Sauuf	Sauuf
Fenugreek	Uluva	Methee	Methee
French Beans	Payar	Flas Beans	Flas Beans
Garlic	Veluthully	Lasum	Thoom
Ginger Root	Injee	Adhruk	Adhruk
Green Chili	Pachamulaku	Hari rchi	Sava Mirchi
Green Gram	Cherupayar	Mung Bean	Mung Bean
Jaggery	Chakkara	Gur	Gur
Lentils	Parippu	Dal	Dal
Mint	Puthina	Phodina	Pudina
Molasses	Sarkara	Gur	Gur
Mustard Seeds	Kaduku	Rai	Rai

KERALA CUISINE

ENGLISH	MALAYALAM	HINDI	PUNJABI
Nutmeg	Jathikka	Jaiphal	Jaiphal
Poppy	Kasakasa	Kuskus	Kuskus
Saffron	Kesari	Kesar	Kesar
Sesame	Ellu	Til	Til
Spinach	Cheera	Palak	Palak
Split Chickpea	Kadala Parippu	Chana Ki Dal	Chana Kidal
Split Black Gram	Uzhunnu	Urad Ki Dal	Mah Kidal
Tamarind	Puli	Imli	Imli
Tapioca	Chowari	Sabudana	Sabudana
Turmeric	Manjal	Huldi	Huldi
Cream of Wheat	Rava	Sooji	Sooji
Yogurt	Thairu	Dahi	Dahi

Dry & Liquid Equivalents

1 Tablespoon	=	3 Teaspoons
2 Tablespoons	=	1 Ounce
8 Tablespoons	=	½ Cup
½ Cup	=	4 Ounces
16 Tablespoons	=	1 Cup
2 Cups	=	1 Pint
2 Pints	=	1 Quart
4 Quarts	=	1 Gallon
Pinch	=	less than 1/8 of a teaspoon

Abbreviations Used

Tbs	Tablespoon
Tsp	Teaspoon
Lb	Pound
Gms	Grams
"	inch

KERALA CUISINE

Tips

Though curries are a prominent part of Indian meals, all curries do not taste alike. They are distinct from state to state. Kerala curries with all the fresh spices give a special aroma and sweetness unknown to other regions. Most of the spices used by the Keralites have some sort of medicinal value. Either they are antiseptic, carminative, or preservative. To make the curries in this recipe book, do not use any kind of curry powder. For best result buy the prescribed spices and grind them separately. You may buy the powder of all spices. When using powder in a recipe, reduce heat to minimum before adding it. Unlike other dishes curries serve best the next day, for it improves upon sitting.

Coconut:
When buying a coconut, make sure that the eyes of the coconut are hard, not soft and moldy. Do not buy a cracked one. Shake them to make sure of the liquid inside. Break the shell and take coconut flesh carefully with a knife. Cut them to small pieces and blend in a food processor or blender. Grated coconut freezes well and defrosts fast. To extract fresh coconut milk, grate the coconut or shred it in a food processor. Pour 1 cup boiled water and grind in the blender for a few seconds. Squeeze out the milk from the pulp. Pour 1 cup more hot water into the pulp and squeeze out milk till the pulp becomes dry. Tinned coconut milk is available in most stores. Before opening the tin shake it well. If the cream is set on the top, mix it thoroughly with the liquid before using.

Ginger Root:
In many of my recipes I use ginger root. It gives a strong

aggressive flavor and also purifies the system. It is good for digestion and improving immunity. Buy the fresh ones from store. Ginger freezes well. Wash, peel off skin, and grate.

Mustard:
It is believed these tiny, dark, round seeds are very good for our digestive system. Add mustard seed to hot oil and cover to pop up. It has a special pungent flavor when popped in oil.

Turmeric:
Though it does not have any strong flavor, is used mainly for its medicinal value and colour. It is also a good skin ointment.

Garlic:
Garlic is an antiseptic rich in vitamins. It has a special flavour when used with fish and meat.

Cinnamon, Star Anise, Cloves, Cardamom, Nutmeg:
All these spices are freshly grown within the reach of every Keralite family. Fresh ground spices taste best. Either powder or whole ones can be bought from the spice stores. They have great health benefits.

Cumin:
Cumin is a good source for vitamin A, C, and E. It fights against cold and digestive problems.

Tamarind:
There are two types of tamarind, fish tamarind, generally known as "thottupuli" and the other "valanpuli". The fish tamarind "thottupuli" gives a special flavor to fish dishes. Both are available in spice stores. You may use lemon juice instead of tamarind. Valanpuli is used to make Rasam and Sambar.

KERALA CUISINE

Atta:
It is a kind of whole wheat flour mixed with other gram flours. This is good for making chappathis, pooris and parottas.

Ghee:
Many of the recipes use ghee instead of butter. Ghee is made by melting butter and allowing the water content to evaporate. Milk solids are separated in the slow heating process. Ghee has several health benefits. It is said to be lactose tolerant since the impurities are removed. However check with your doctor before consuming it. It is rich in vitamins and can stay longer than butter. It is called clarified butter. It has a nutty special flavour.

☞ Since many of the dishes have a rice base, people who are allergic to milk and wheat products will find something interesting and new to try.

KERALA CUISINE

Table of Contents

Introduction i
Preface iii
Dry & Liquid Equivalents v
Abbreviations Used vi
Tips vii

BREADS 2
   BATTURA (PUFFY BREAD) 2
   MASALA DOSA (STUFFED PANCAKES) 4
   IDLI (STEAMED RICE DUMPLINGS) 7
   DOSA (SAVORY PANCAKES) 9
   STUFFED PAPER ROAST 11
   PATHIRI (RICE PANCAKE) 13
   KOZHUKATTA (Stuffed Rice Dumplings) 14
   PALAPPAM (SAVORY MILK PANCAKES) 15
   VELLAYAPPAM (RICE STEAMED PANCAKE) 17
   VATTAYAPPAM (STEAMEDRICE CAKE) 18
   CHAPPATHI 19
   POORI (FRIED INDIAN BREAD) 21
   PAROTTA (FLAKY BREAD) 22
   STUFFED PAROTTA-ONION PAROTTA 24
   POTATO PAROTTA 25
   NAN (BAKED PAROTTA) 26
   UPPUMA (CREAM OF WHEAT) 28

MEAT 31
   CHICKEN CURRY (South Indian Style) 31
   SAVORY CHICKEN CURRY 33
   STEAMED CHILI CHICKEN CURRY 34
   GINGER CHICKEN 35
   BAKED CHICKEN 37
   SIMPLE FRIED CHICKEN 38
   CHICKEN STEW 39
   SPICY FRIED CHICKEN 41

KERALA CUISINE

CHICKEN IN COCONUT MILK	42
CHICKEN BREAST DELICIOUS	43
THANDOORI CHICKEN	44
CRISPY BAKED CHICKEN LEGS	45
RAISIN CHICKEN	45
MANGO CHICKEN (SWEET AND SOUR CHICKEN)	47
BUTTER CHICKEN	48
FRIED DUCK	50
FAVOURITE DUCK FRY	51
DUCK ROAST	52
DUCK POTATO STEW	53
TURKEY TIT BIT	55
SPICY TURKEY	56
MEAT CUTLET	57
CHILI BEEF FRY	59
CHILI GINGER BEEF CURRY	60
SPICY BEEF FRY	61
LIVER FRY	62
EASY MEAT DISH	63
KERALA BEEF	64
FRIED BEEF	66
HAMBURGER MEAT FRY	67
MEAT VEGETABLE STEW	68
RED MEAT CURRY	69
LAMB ROAST	71
LAMB BROWNIE	72
BRAIN ROAST	73
PORK VINDALOO	74
PORK FRY	75
EGGS	77
EGG MASALA ROAST	77
EGG CARROT DISH	79
EGG COCONUT DISH	79
TASTY EGG PATTIES	81

KERALA CUISINE

PRAWNS AND EGG 82

RICE 83
CHICKEN BIRIYANI 83
CHICKEN BIRIYANI 2 85
BAKED BIRIANI 88
PLAIN FRIED RICE 90
LAMB BIRIANI 91
VEGETABLE & PRAWN FRIED RICE 93
SIMPLE FRIED RICE 95
QUICK VEGETABLE BIRIANI 96
CARROT RICE 98
THAIRU SADHAM (YOGURT RICE) 99
LEMON RICE 100
CHILI RICE 101

FISH 103
FISH CUTLET 103
KERALA FISH CUTLETS 104
FRIED FISH 106
COUNTRY STYLE FISH FRY 107
BAKED FISH 108
FISH IN COCONUT MILK 109
STUFFED FISH 110
FISH MOLEE 111
RED FISH CURRY (MEEN CURRY) 112
FISH AND PEAS STEW 113
COCONUT FISH (MEEN PEERA) 114
FRIED FISH 115
FRIED FISH CURRY 116
FISH BROWNIE 117
BAKED FISH CRUNCH 118

SHRIMPS, LOBSTER, CRAB 119

KERALA CUISINE

SHRIMP/PRAWN CURRY	119
SHRIMP CHILI FRY	121
YUMMY SHRIMP FRY	122
SHRIMP MASALA	124
LOBSTER FRY	125
CURRIED LOBSTER	126
BAKED LOBSTER	127
FAVOURITE CRAB DISH	129
CRAB COCONUT CURRY	130
VEGETABLES	**132**
BROCCOLI MUSHROOM DISH	132
STRING BEANS AND POTATOES	133
QUICK VEGETABLE CUTLET	134
LENTIL DISH	135
MUNG BEANS CURRY	136
SAMBAR (VEGETABLE CURRY)	138
BROWN CHICK PEAS	140
GINGER CURRY	141
RASAM OR MULAGUTHANNY	143
CASHEW NUT CURRY	146
AVIAL	148
EGG PLANT FRY	149
QUICK EGG PLANT FRY	150
OKRA STIR-FRY	151
CABBAGE THORAN	152
SPICY POTATO FRY	153
CAULIFLOWER CURRY	154
SPICY MASHED POTATO	156
VEGETABLE CUTLET (CLASSIC STYLE)	157
SPINACH CUTLET	158
BITTER GOURD FRY	160
PUMPKIN DISH	161
PLANTAIN FINGERS	163
MUSHROOM DISH	164

KERALA CUISINE

MUSHROOM CURRY	165
PUMPKIN LEAVES THORAN	166

PICKLES 168
SWEET LEMON PICKLE	168
LEMON PICKLE	170
RAISINS LEMON PICKLE	171
MANGO PICKLE I	172
MANGO PICKLE II	173
PRAWN PICKLE	174
LOBSTER PICKLE	175
MEAT PICKLE	176
BITTER GOURD PICKLE	177
CARROT PICKLE	178
EGGPLANT PICKLE	179
GARLIC PICKLE	180
FISH PICKLE	180

CHUTNEYS 183
CARROT CHUTNEY	183
TOMATO CHUTNEY	184
COCONUT CHUTNEY 1 (FOR DOSA & IDLY)	185
COCONUT CHUTNEY 2 (SAMMENDY)	186
MANGO CHUTNEY	187
MINT CHUTNEY	187
BAKED FISH CHUTNEY	188
FISH MANGO CHUTNEY	189
BAKED CHUTNEY POWDER (SAMMENDY PODI)	189

CHIPS 191
POPPADUMS	191
TAPIOCA WAFER	192
BANANA CHIPS	192

KERALA CUISINE

SALADS 193
   TOMATO ONION SALAD 193
   CABBAGE COCONUT SALAD 194
   CUCUMBER SALAD 195
   PRAWNS SALAD 196

SNACKS 198
   BAKED SAMOSA 198
   UZHUNNU VADA (URAD DAL VADA) 200
   PARIPPU VADA 202
   CREAM OF WHEAT DELIGHT 203
   PLANTAIN DELIGHT (ETHEKA APPAM) 204
   UNNIAPPAM 205
   BANANA UNNIAPPAM 206
   PLANTAIN FRITTERS 207
   VEGETABLE PATTIES 208
   PEANUT CRISPS 209
   SESAME BALLS 210
   GULAB JAMAN 211
   BAKED BANANA PUFFS 212
   PEA FLOUR FUDGE 213
   RICE FUDGE 214
   CREAM OF WHEAT LADU 215
   CREAM OF WHEAT COCONUT PASTRY 216
   MEAT PUFFS 217
   ONION PAKKODA 218
   POTATO BHAJI 219
   BONDA 220
   CRISPY COOKIES (MURUKKU) 221
   WHITE HALVA 222
   CARROT HALVA 223
   PUMPKIN HALVA 224
   BLACK HALVA 225
   RICE HALVA 226

KERALA CUISINE

CAKES & COOKIES 228
  PERFECT CAKE 228
  JAGGERY CAKE 229
  CARAMEL CAKE 230
  SPICY WHEAT FLOUR CAKE 231
  EASY COCOA CAKE 232
  FOUR EGGS CAKE 233
  NO EGG CAKE 234
  CARROT APPLE CAKE 235
  DATES CAKE 236
  FRUIT CAKE 237
  NANKATAI 239
  GINGER BISCUITS 240

COOKIES 241
  OATMEAL COOKIES 241
  PEANUT COOKIES 242
  QUICK APPLE PIE 243

SWEET DISHES (PAYASAM) 244
  VERMICELLI DESSERT 244
  CREAM OF WHEAT DESSERT 246
  RICE DESSERT 247
  MUNG BEANS DESSERT 248
  ADA PRATHAMAN 249
  FRUIT SALAD 250

BREADS

BREADS

BREADS

BATTURA (PUFFY BREAD)

1. All Purpose Flour — 2 cups
2. Egg — 1
3. Butter (softened) — 2 Tbs
4. Milk — ½ cup
5. Instant Yeast — 1 tsp
6. Salt — ½ tsp

   Vegetable Oil for frying

PREPARATION:

Measure 2 cups of flour into a bowl. Add salt. Blend softened butter. Combine beaten egg, milk and instant yeast. Add this to the flour little by little and mix. Knead to make a soft and pliable dough. Cover with a plastic wrap or a damp cloth and keep for 2-3 hours to rise. After dough has doubled in size take out and divide into ten small egg size balls. Roll into round, thin pastries. Coat with flour if they tend to stick while rolling. Heat oil in a deep fryer and when sizzling hot put these rolled out pastries in one by one. It will sizzle, sink under the oil and come up with bubbles. With a spoon, gently press on the top. This will cause it to puff up. Turn over. Leave for a few seconds and drain. Serve hot with chicken stew.

Battura can be kept in the fridge, covered in foil for up to a week. Spread in the oven and reheat for 6-10 minutes at 350 F, or microwave each for 10 seconds.

BREADS

BREADS

MASALA DOSA (STUFFED PANCAKES)

1. Rice Flour   2 cups
2. Urad Flour   ¾ cup
3. Cooked Rice   ½ cup
4. Yeast (Instant)   ½ tsp
5. Baking Powder   ½ tsp
   Salt to taste

FILLING

1. Potato   3 cups cooked & pureed
2. Carrots   2 cups grated
3. Turnip   1 cup
4. Celery   1 cup cut crosswise, thin
5. Green Peas   1 cup
6. Ginger root   1 Tbs grated
7. Onion   1 cup chopped
8. Black Mustard   ½ tsp
9. Green Chili Pepper 1 chopped (optional)
10. Green Pepper   1 chopped
11. Turmeric   ½ tsp
12. Red Chili   1 broken to 6
    or Chili Powder   ½ tsp
13. Coriander Powder   ½ tsp
14. Oil   4 Tbs
    Salt to taste

BREADS

PREPARATION:

Mix yeast with rice flour. Pour 1½ cups warm water into urad flour and blend in a blender along with cooked rice. Set aside. Blend the rice flour with 1½ cups water for 1 minute. Combine both batters and keep for 12 hours. Add salt and baking powder. Heat a griddle or non-stick frying pan, brush oil and pour one big spoonful of batter in the centre and with the spoon spread the batter thin and circular like a very thin pancake. If the griddle is very hot, one cannot spread batter thinly. So after brushing with oil sprinkle a little water on the griddle before pouring in the batter. Cook in medium heat. Pour a little oil or butter around and the centre of dosa (pancake) to make it crisp. When fully cooked, place filling in a line from one end to another of the dosa. Fold opposite sides to the centre to hold filling in the middle. Serve hot.

FILLING

Sauté mustard in 2 tablespoon oil and when mustard pops up, add onion, ginger and chilies. When they turn soft add red chilies. Reduce heat and add coriander and turmeric. Add vegetables. Stir and sauté till they become soft (2-3 minutes). Add mashed potatoes and ¼ cup water. Bring to a boil while stirring and turn off heat. Make dosas, stuff with filling and serve with sambar and coconut chutney. You can stuff 15 dosas with this filling.

BREADS

Other vegetables like beets, cauliflower, broccoli, beans, peas, etc. can be used. Instead of vegetables left-over meat or ground beef can be substituted.

BREADS

IDLI (STEAMED RICE DUMPLINGS)

This is a very nutritious and tasty dish. An egg poaching mold can be used for steaming Idlies. The right batter is the secret for making good Idlies. Rich in protein, carbs, & vitamins.

1. Rice Flour   2 cup
2. Par Boiled Rice   1 cup
3. Split black gram   1¼ cup
   (Urad dal)
4. Yogurt   2 Tbs
5. Instant Yeast   ½ tsp
   Salt to taste
   Oil to brush the mold

PREPARATION:

Soak separate parboiled rice and black gram in warm water for 4 hours. Wash and grind rice in a blender to a coarse paste with 1 cup of water. Blend rice flour with yeast to a soft batter adding enough water (¾cup). In 1½ - 2 cups water blend black gram to a very fine texture. Pour it into the rice paste and mix well. Add 2 tablespoons yogurt. Combine. The batter should have a dropping consistency like a cake batter. Keep it covered overnight in a warm place. After 12 hours it will double. Add 1½ tsp salt. With a pastry brush, brush a little oil in each mold to avoid sticking. Pour into each mold 3 tablespoon of batter and steam for 5-8 minutes. Remove and cool for 2 minutes. Gently take out the cooked idlies from the mold with a

BREADS

serving knife starting from the sides to the centre. Serve hot with coconut chutney and sambar (vegetable curry).

BREADS

DOSA (SAVORY PANCAKES)

1. Rice Flour   1 ½ cups
2. Par Boiled Rice   ¼ cup
3. Cooked Rice   2 Tbs
4. Urad Dal   1/2 cup
5. Baking Soda   a pinch
6. Salt to taste
   Oil or butter to brush the griddle

PREPARATION:

Soak rice and urad in warm water for 4 hours. Blend both to a very fine paste adding enough water. Combine cooked rice with rice flour, add water and blend to a smooth paste. Add enough water to form a light running consistency. Add a pinch of baking soda. Cover and keep overnight. Season with salt. Heat a non-stick frying pan or griddle, brush a little oil and pour a big spoonful of batter in the centre. With the back of the spoon spread the batter from the center towards the sides in a circular motion, making it as thin as possible. Dot a little oil or butter over the dosa to make it crisp. Cover and cook. Fold one end to the other side. If the inside is not cooked turn over and cook for a few seconds.

BREADS

Extra Recipe:

BREADS

STUFFED PAPER ROAST

Quick, easy, tasty.

1. Rice Flour   2 cups
2. Eggs   2
3. Milk   3 cups
4. Baking Powder   1 tsp
5. Caraway Seeds   1 tsp (optional)
   Oil to brush griddle
   Salt to taste

PREPARATION:

Blend rice flour with milk for 2 minutes. Beat eggs well and add in. Add baking powder, caraway seeds and salt. Pour 1 big spoon of batter in the centre of a heated nonstock frying pan and spread as thin as paper from the centre towards the sides to form a large round pancake. Dot a little butter over the pancake. It will be cooked within 20-25 seconds. Remove pancake from heat then put filling in the middle and roll out.

Filling can be of either vegetables or meat. Instead of stuffing this can be served with some curries like chicken stew. Kids love them plain with butter and honey.

VEGETABLE STUFFING
1. Cabbage   1 cup shredded
2. Carrot   1 cup diced
3. Broccoli   1 cup diced
4. Onion   1 cup sliced

BREADS

5. Green chili   1 deseeded, chopped
6. Butter   2 Tbs
7. Chili Sauce   ¼ cup
   Salt to taste

PREPARATION:

Sauté onion in butter till soft. Add the remaining vegetables. Stir fry for 3 minutes. Add chili sauce. Stir well and use as filling for the paper roast.

MEAT STUFFING

1. Left-over meat   2 cups, boneless
2. Mushrooms   1 cup chopped
3. Onion   1 cup
4. Cinnamon Powder   ¾ tsp
5. Chili Sauce   ¼ cup
6. Butter or Oil   2 Tbs
   Salt to taste

PREPARATION:

Debone meat and shred with a fork. Sauté onion and mushrooms in 2 tablespoon butter till soft. Add cinnamon powder. Add meat and sauté for a while. Add chili sauce. Mix well and use as filling.

BREADS

PATHIRI (RICE PANCAKE)

1. Rice Flour   1 cup
2. Coconut Milk   2 cup
3. Butter   1 Tbs
   Salt to taste

PREPARATION:

Dry fry rice flour for 2-3 minutes stirring well. Boil 1 cup coconut milk in a pot with salt. Add rice flour and stir. When it becomes cool make small lemon size balls. Roll out as thin and round as possible. Heat a griddle or non-stick frying pan and cook this for 20 to 30 seconds. Turn over and cook till the small bubbles on both sides turn light brown. Combine 1 tablespoon butter with 1 cup coconut milk and heat the mixture (do not boil). Pour little by little on both sides of each cooked pathiri. Serve with lamb curry.

Extra Recipe:

KOZHUKATTA (Stuffed Rice Dumplings)

1. Rice Flour   2 cups
2. Coconut   1 cup
3. Brown Sugar   ½ cup
4. Lemon Juice   1 tsp
5. Cardamom Powder   ½ tsp
6. Milk   1 cup
7. Yogurt   1 Tbs
   Salt to taste

PREPARATION:

Dry fry rice flour on medium heat 2 to 3 minutes. Turn off heat. Combine sugar and fresh grated coconut. Sprinkle in lemon juice and cardamom powder. Mix and set aside. Make a soft dough with rice flour, 1 cup hot milk and 1 tablespoon yogurt. Knead well. Make small egg size balls. Flatten each ball and stuff 1 tsp of the coconut mixture in the middle and seal by bringing the sides together to form a ball. Boil water in a big container and keep the balls in the steamer. (Keep steamer tray above water level). Steam it for 10-12 minutes. Serve hot.

BREADS

PALAPPAM (SAVORY MILK PANCAKES)

A favourite Kerala dish - very addictive.

1. Rice Flour   3 cups
3. Cooked Rice   ¼ cup
4. Coconut Milk   2 cups (one can)
5. Sugar   4 Tbs
6. Instant Yeast   1½ tsp
   Salt to taste

PREPARATION:

Make a paste of 1 tablespoon rice flour and ½ cup water by bringing it to a boil while stirring continuously. When thickened, turn off heat. Combine rice flour, coconut milk, cooked rice, rice paste, sugar, salt, and yeast. Add 2 cups of water and blend all to a fine smooth batter. Set aside for 2 hours. Keep the batter in the fridge overnight. Heat a wok, brush oil and pour one large spoonful of batter in the centre of the wok. Hold the two handles of the wok and tilt it in a circular motion for the batter to form a thin round lacy layer. Cover for a minute. When sides are light brown and there is no uncooked batter in the centre the pancake is ready. Take out and set on a plate. Brush the wok with oil again and repeat the process. A non-stick pan is better for this.

Savory milk pancakes can be eaten as a main dish along with curried vegetables or meat, (chicken stew or potato stew). Dribble fresh coconut milk and honey

BREADS

on the hot appam for a mouth-watering treat.
For a richer texture & taste use basmati rice soaked in water for four hours and blend with coconut milk, sugar, rice paste, and yeast.

VELLAYAPPAM (RICE STEAMED PANCAKE)

1. Rice flour   2 cups
2. Coconut grated   1½ cup
3. Cumin Seeds   ½ tsp
4. Sugar   3 Tbs
5. Instant Yeast   1 tsp
   Salt to taste

PREPARATION:

Heat 2 tablespoon rice flour and 1 cup water in a saucepan, stirring constantly. Bring to a boil. When rice flour is cooked and thickened remove from heat. Grind coconut and cumin seeds along with 1 cup water to a coarse paste. Combine rice flour, rice paste, yeast, and sugar. Add water and blend to a smooth, thick batter. Mix with coconut. Set aside for 2 hours. Keep the batter in the fridge overnight. By morning it will be well risen. Add salt. Heat a griddle or non-stick frying pan, brush with oil or butter and pour one spoon full of batter in the centre. Make a small round shape (about 1/8" thick) with the back of the spoon. Cover and cook for 30 to 40 seconds. Remove and place on a large plate. Repeat the process. Serve with meat stew. Vellayappam can be eaten plain as they are.

BREADS

VATTAYAPPAM (STEAMEDRICE CAKE)

1. Rice Flour — 2 cups
2. Coconut — 1½ cup grated
3. Yeast — 1 tsp
4. Cooked Rice — ¼ cup
5. Egg White — 1
6. Sugar — 4 Tbs
7. Raisins — ½ cup
8. Cumin Seeds — ½ tsp
9. Onion — ¼ cup chopped
   Water — 2 ½ cups
   Salt to taste

PREPARATION:

Heat 2 tablespoon rice flour and ½ cup water stirring continuously. Bring to a boil. Turn off heat. Make a coarse paste of coconut, cumin and onion. Add the remaining flour, cooked rice paste, yeast, sugar and water and blend together for 2 minutes. Leave till the dough is doubled. Keep in fridge. Add salt and one well beaten egg white. Brush two pans with butter, pour in batter to 1" thickness. Steam in a steamer for 15-20 minutes. After 10 minutes put raisins on top of the cake here and there. Cover and continue cooking. Insert a tooth pick in the centre, if nothing sticks to it, the cake is done. Remove from pan, cool and cut. Steam the rest of the cakes in the same way.

BREADS

CHAPPATHI

1. Atta Flour — 1 cup
2. All Purpose Flour — 3 Tbs
3. Vegetable Oil — 2 Tbs
4. All Purpose Flour — ¼ cup for dusting
5. Water — ¼ - ½ cup
6. Oil for brushing
   Salt to taste

PREPARATION:

Combine flours in a bowl. Mix with vegetable oil and salt. Add water and knead well to form a soft, firm dough. Cover with plastic wrap or a damp cloth and set aside for 1 to 2 hours. Divide dough into small egg size balls. Dust each one with a little flour and roll out to a thin, round pastry. If chappathi becomes sticky coat with flour and continue rolling. Heat a griddle or skillet and cook the chappathi for a minute first few seconds on high heat, then on medium heat. Cook each side for 30 seconds. Turn over. Small bubbles will form. Brush a little oil on both sides. Press with a spatula on the centre and sides. Chappathi will puff up. Turn again and press with spatula. When it turns golden yellow with brown spots, it is ready to be taken out from the griddle. Repeat the same process with the remaining rolled out chapattis. Serve hot with beef curry.

> *Chappathi can be made several hours before or even the night before and reheated on tin foil for 8-10 minutes at 350 F. Or microwave each for 10-15 seconds.*

BREADS

Extra Recipe:

BREADS

POORI (FRIED INDIAN BREAD)

A tasty and easily prepared dish.

1. All Purpose Flour — 1 cup
2. Cream of Wheat — ¼ cup
3. Vegetable Oil — 2 Tbs
4. Water — ½ cup
5. Oil to fry
   Salt to taste

PREPARATION:

Pour ¼ cup water into a bowl and add cream of wheat. Add flour, salt and vegetable oil. Mix oil with the flour. Add in the rest of the water and knead for 5 to 7 minutes to form a soft dough. Keep covered for about 1 to 2 hours. Make small 1" balls. Dust flour on the rolling board, roll each ball into a thin round pastry. Heat 1-2 cups oil in a deep fryer and deep fry each one. Gently press the top with a slotted spoon as it sizzles and rises. The pressing will make it to puff up like a ball. Gently turn over. Fry for a few seconds. Drain, pat with a paper towel and serve hot.

BREADS

PAROTTA (FLAKY BREAD)

1. All Purpose Flour   ½ cup
2. Atta Flour   1 cup
3. White Bread Slice   1
4. Vegetable Oil   3 Tbs
5. Margarine   2 Tbs
6. Water   ½-¾ cup
   Salt to taste

PREPARATION:

Soak a slice of bread in water. Squeeze out the water, break the bread into small pieces and add to the flour. Add salt and oil. Mix. Add water gradually to make a soft pliable dough by kneading for 3-5 minutes. Cover the dough with plastic wrap and set aside for at least ½ an hour. Divide the dough into lemon size balls. Dust flour on the rolling board. Coat the balls with the flour and roll out a thin round pastry. Shake off the excess flour from the top of the pastry. Brush 1 tsp margarine on top of the pastry. Fold in half. Brush the top with a little margarine again. Fold to form a triangular shape. Coat this with flour again and roll out a flat pastry. Heat a griddle or skillet until very hot. Place the rolled pastry and cook each side for 20-30 seconds. Light brown spots will start appearing. Brush oil or butter on top. Turn over and brush oil again. Gently press sides and centre so that they will puff up. When light brown spots become darker on both sides, remove from heat. Repeat the process till all are done. Serve hot.

BREADS

It is very good to eat as itself. Best side dish is chicken potato stew. Terrific taste with honey and butter. Use sandwich meat and cheese for a treat.

BREADS

STUFFED PAROTTA-ONION PAROTTA

This is one of my favourite dishes. Try, you will like it!

1. All Purpose Flour   2 cups
2. Vegetable Oil   ¼ cup
3. Baking Soda   ½ tsp
4. Sugar   1 tsp
5. Egg (optional)   1
6. Onion   2 cups chopped
7. Water   ½ cup
8. Oil to brush
   Salt   ¾ tsp or to taste

PREPARATION:

Mix flour with baking soda. Mix in the oil. Add sugar, salt and a beaten egg. Add in warm water gradually and make a smooth pliable dough. Set aside for one hour. Cut onions thin and chop. Divide the dough into 16 small balls. Roll out two thin pastries. Spread a layer of chopped onion on top of one of the pastries. Cover with another pastry. Seal edges very well. Sprinkle flour on top and gently roll out again. Carefully turn over and roll out as thin as possible. The onion may crush a bit and sometimes will break through the pastry. Dust off the extra flour on the pastry by turning between the palms. Place parotta on a heated skillet or griddle stone. After a few seconds turn over. Brush oil on top and pour a little oil through the slits in the parotta. Turn over again and brush oil on the top. Cook till brown spots appear on both sides. Gently press the sides and uncooked spots with the spatula

BREADS

while cooking. Serve hot. Chick Pea curry and lemon pickle go well with it. You can make 8 parottas with the above recipe.

Adding chili powder and grated fresh ginger to the onions produce a strong aggressive flavour.

POTATO PAROTTA

1. Parotta dough as in preceding recipe
2. Potato   2 cups cooked, mashed
3. Black Gram   1 tsp (Urad Dal)
4. Onion   ¼ cup
5. Chili Powder   ½ tsp
6. Tomato   ½ cup cut in cubes
7. Vegetable Oil   1 cup
   Salt to taste

PREPARATION:

Sauté mustard and split black gram in 3 Tbs hot oil. Add chopped onion and stir fry until soft. Reduce heat and add chili powder. Add cubed tomatoes and cook till soft. Mix with peeled, cooked, and mashed potatoes stirring well. Season with salt. Set aside. Divide parotta dough into small balls. Make a thin round pastry. Spread a layer of mashed potato on top. Cut from centre to one edge. Take the cut side and roll the whole pastry up like a cone. Keep the cone vertically and gently press from the top to the bottom forming a plate. Dust the board and roll out a thin parotta. Dust off excess flour. Heat frying pan or

BREADS

griddle stone and cook as onion parotta.

Any vegetable can be used for a stuffing.

NAN (BAKED PAROTTA)

1. All Purpose Flour — 2 cups
2. Baking Powder — ½ tsp
3. Instant yeast — 1 tsp
4. Plain Yogurt — ½ cup
5. Egg — 1
6. Milk — ¼ - ½ cup
7. Sugar — 1 tsp (optional)
8. Margarine — 1 Tbs
9. Sesame seeds — 2 tsp
   Salt — ½ tsp or to taste

PREPARATION:

Combine flour, salt, sugar, baking powder, and yeast. Rub in margarine. Beat egg well and add to the flour followed by yogurt and warmed milk. Knead well. Cover with a plastic wrap and leave for 2 hours to become double in size. Knead again and divide dough to 6 to 7 balls. Roll out into 1/8 " in thickness or flatten with hand. Press sesame seeds on top. Keep on baking sheets and bake in a hot oven (450 F) for 2-3 minutes or till it is puffed and cooked. Serve hot.

BREADS

UPPUMA (CREAM OF WHEAT)

1. Cream of Wheat   1 cup
2. Onion   2 Tbs chopped
3. Ginger Root   ¼" piece chopped
4. Mustard Seeds   ½ tsp
5. Split lentils   1 tsp
6. Urad Dal   1 tsp
7. Green Chili   1 chopped
8. Cashews, Raisins   ½ cup
9. Curry Leaves   5
10. Butter   ¼ cup
11. Vegetable Oil   3 Tbs
    Salt to taste

PREPARATION:

Heat butter and oil together. When sizzling hot add mustard and allow to pop. Add lentils and urad dal and stir for a few seconds. Immediately add sliced onion followed by ginger, chili, and curry leaves. Add broken cashews and raisins. Stir till cashews turn golden. Add cream of wheat and salt. Stir fry for 2 minutes. Meanwhile boil 1½ cup water in a kettle. Reduce heat and pour this boiling water into the cream of wheat mixture stirring constantly. Sprinkle 2 tsp sugar and stir to break all lumps. Sprinkle some more water and cover and keep on minimum heat for 1 to 2 minutes. Uncover, stir well and serve.

BREADS

MEAT

MEAT

CHICKEN CURRY (South Indian Style)

1. Chicken — 4 lbs
2. Onion — 2 (peeled, chopped)
3. Ginger Root — 2" long (grated)
4. Garlic — 5 cloves (crushed)
5. Green Chili — 2 (chopped)
6. Chili Powder — 2 tsp
7. Coriander Powder — 2½ Tbs
8. Cloves Powder — ½ tsp
9. Cinnamon Powder — ½ tsp
10. Fennel Seed Powder — ½ tsp
11. Tomato — 3 (medium)
12. Mustard Seeds — 1 tsp
13. Curry Leaves — 8
14. Butter or Oil — ¼ cup
15. Coconut milk — 1 cup
16. Potatoes — 3 medium, peeled, halved

Salt to taste

PREPARATION:

Remove skin and cut chicken into neat pieces. Peel and halve the potatoes. Add grated ginger, crushed garlic, ½ cup sliced onion, and chopped green chili. Sprinkle with salt. Cover and cook for 15 minutes. Meanwhile melt butter in a skillet and pop mustard seeds over high heat. Stir in the remaining sliced onion and stir fry till golden brown. Add curry leaves and reduce heat to minimum. Mix ingredients 6-10 in a small bowl with ¼ cup water and add in. Simmer for

MEAT

a minute. Finely chop tomatoes and add. Increase heat and stir fry till tomatoes become soft. Mix with chicken. Bring to a boil and simmer for 3 minutes. Pour whipping cream or coconut milk. Check the tenderness of the chicken and the seasoning. Combine well and serve.

Extra Recipe:

MEAT

SAVORY CHICKEN CURRY

1. Chicken Joints — 4 lbs
2. Onion — 2 (one sliced thinly)
3. Ginger Root — 2" long
4. Garlic — 4 cloves
5. Green Chili Pepper — 2 seeds removed
6. Chili Powder — 2 tsp
8. Cardamom Powder — 2 pods
9. Cloves Powder — ¾ tsp
10. Cinnamon Powder — ½ tsp
11. Fennel Seed Powder — 1 tsp
12. Butter — 4 Tbs
13. Mustard Seeds — 1 tsp
14. Curry Leaves — 10
15. Yogurt — 2 cups

Salt to taste.

PREPARATION:

Make a puree of ginger, garlic, green pepper, and one onion in a blender. Mix with ingredients 6 to 11. Season with salt and yogurt. Marinate the chicken pieces for 1 hour. Cover and cook for 15-20 minutes over medium heat. Heat butter or oil in a frying pan and pop mustard seeds over high heat. Stir in the remaining sliced onion and sauté till lightly brown. Add curry leaves and stir fry for a few seconds. Mix with cooked chicken. Serve hot with any kind of bread or pancake or chappathi.

STEAMED CHILI CHICKEN CURRY

1. Chicken — 4 lbs cut into cubes
2. Chili Powder — 2 Tbs
3. Garlic — 8 cloves
4. Tomatoes — 6 finely chopped
5. Tomato paste — 3 tsp
6. Onion — 3 thinly sliced
7. Star Anise — 1 whole or powder
8. Vegetable Oil — ½ cup
   Salt to taste

PREPARATION:

Blend onion (one) and garlic in ½ cup water. Mix with chili, tomato paste, salt and star anise. Smear the chicken pieces and steam the whole mixture for ½ an hour in a double boiler. Drain the chicken pieces from the soup and fry it in butter or oil till lightly brown. Fry the thinly sliced onion in the remaining butter till golden brown. Add the soup and fried onion to the chicken and bring to a boil. Simmer for a few minutes till gravy is thick.

MEAT

GINGER CHICKEN

1.	Chicken	4 lbs
2.	Potato	3 medium, cut in halves
3.	Ginger Root	2" long, grated
4.	Green Chili	2 chopped
5.	Onion	3 chopped
6.	Chili Powder	1 tsp
7.	Coriander Powder	2½ Tbs
8.	Black Pepper	1 tsp
9.	Fennel Seed Powder	2 tsp
10.	Turmeric	½ tsp
11.	Lemon Juice	1 Tbs
12.	Curry Leaves	7
13.	Butter	¼ cup
14.	Yogurt	2 cups
	Salt to taste	

PREPARATION:

Discard skin and cut the meat into bite size pieces. Melt butter in a heavy bottomed pot over a high heat and sauté onion for 2 minutes. Add potatoes, green chilies and curry leaves and stir for further 2 minutes. Reduce heat and add ingredients 6-10. Stir fry for a few seconds and stir in grated ginger. Sprinkle salt. Add chicken to the pot. Pour in yogurt and mix well. Cover and cook over medium heat for 20 minutes. As the chicken becomes tender, sprinkle on lemon juice. Turn the chicken occasionally to avoid sticking. It is a delicious curry for rice, corn, bread, etc.

If more gravy is required add half cup of butter milk when the chicken is half cooked.

MEAT

Fresh ginger can be frozen.

Extra Recipe:

MEAT

BAKED CHICKEN

This is a very good dish to try.

1. Chicken   4 lbs cut 2"long
2. Potatoes   4 peeled, halved
3. Onion   1 sliced
4. Ginger Root   2" long
5. Garlic   8 cloves
6. Tomatoes   4 medium
7. Raisins   ¼ cup
8. Coriander Powder   2 Tbs
9. Chili Powder   1 tsp
10. Cloves Powder   ½ tsp
11. Cinnamon Powder   ½ tsp
12. Fennel Seed Powder ½ tsp
13. Star Anise Powder ½ tsp or 1 whole star
14. Milk   1 cup
15. Whipping Cream   ½ cup
16. Cashews   10 (cut into halves)
17. Butter   2 Tbs
    Salt according to taste

PREPARATION:

Discard skin and cut the chicken to neat pieces. Make a fine paste of ingredients 3-7 in a blender, gradually adding the milk. Mix with items 8-13. Season with salt. In a baking dish arrange chicken and potatoes. Pour the marinade over. Add broken cashews. Dot the top with butter and bake till the chicken is tender for about 40 to 45 minutes at 375^0 F. Pour the cream over, stir well and remove from the oven before boiling. Serve hot with buns, breads or poori.

SIMPLE FRIED CHICKEN

1. Chicken   4 lbs cut 2" long
2. Turmeric   ½ tsp
3. Onion   1
4. Ginger Root   2" long
5. Garlic   9 cloves
6. Black Pepper   2 tsp
7. Lemon Juice   3 tsp
   Oil for deep frying
   Salt to taste

PREPARATION:

Make a fine paste of ingredients 2-8 in a blender. Season with salt. Marinate chicken pieces for 1 hour. Heat oil in a skillet and deep fry the chicken till golden

MEAT

brown. Drain on paper towels.

CHICKEN STEW

Make once, you will be addictive to this great taste!

1. Chicken — 4 lbs cut 2" long
2. Potatoes — 3 medium peeled, halved
3. Milk — 3 ½ cups
4. Onion — 3 cut in wedges
5. Green Chili — 2 thinly chopped
6. Ginger Root — 2" long grated
7. Garlic — 8 cloves grated
8. Cloves — 6 whole ones
9. Cinnamon — 2 sticks 2" long
10. Cardamom — 8 pods
11. Black Pepper — ½ tsp
12. Coriander Powder — 2 tsp
13. Fennel Seed Powder — 1 tsp
14. Lemon Juice — 3 Tbs
15. Curry Leaves — 20
16. Corn Flour — 1 Tbs
17. Vegetable Oil — ¼ - ½ cup
18. Whipping Cream — 1 cup

Salt to taste

PREPARATION:

Heat butter or oil in a heavy bottomed pot. Sauté onion, garlic, ginger, and green chili for 2- 3 minutes. Reduce heat and add curry leaves, whole cloves, cinnamon, and cardamom. Stir for 2 minutes. Add coriander powder, black pepper and fennel seed powder stirring constantly. Bring in chicken pieces.

MEAT

Stir fry for 3 minutes. Add halved potatoes. Season with salt. Add 2 cups of milk. Cover and cook over medium heat for 15 minutes. Stir at times to avoid sticking. Dribble lemon juice. When the chicken is almost tender mix the corn flour with the remaining milk and pour in. Allow the stew to boil. Simmer for 2 minutes. Add cream. Boil and Serve

"One day the little chicks asked their mother "mama why we don't have names like the humans?" Mom replied, "Don't worry my children, we get our names after we die, we are called "chicken tandoori, chicken delicious, chicken fry, chicken curry etc."

MEAT

SPICY FRIED CHICKEN

1. Chicken — 4 lbs cut into 2" pieces
2. Onion — 2
3. Ginger Root — 2" long
4. Garlic — 5 cloves
4. Chili Powder — 1 Tbs
5. Coriander Powder — 1 Tbs
6. Cloves Powder — ½ tsp
7. Cinnamon Powder — ½ tsp
8. Fennel Seed Powder — 1 tsp
9. Tomato Paste — 2 tsp
10. Mint Leaves — 2 sprigs
11. Oil for frying — ½ cup
12. Coriander leaves for garnishing
    Salt to taste

PREPARATION:

Blend ingredients 2-10 to a fine puree in a blender by adding ½ cup water. Sprinkle salt. Smear chicken pieces and cook till all the water evaporates. Cut one onion into thin wedges and sauté in oil or butter. Add chicken pieces and fry till both sides turn golden brown. Garnish with coriander leaves before serving.

MEAT

CHICKEN IN COCONUT MILK

1. Chicken — 4 lbs cut into small pieces
2. Onion — 2 medium chopped
3. Garlic — 4 cloves crushed
4. Ginger Root — 2" long grated
5. Green Chili Pepper — 4 deseeded
6. Cloves Powder — ½ tsp
7. Cinnamon Powder — ½ tsp
8. Poppy Seed Powder — ½ tsp
9. Fennel Seed Powder — 1 tsp
10. Black Pepper — 1 tsp
11. Turmeric — ½ tsp
12. Butter — 3 Tbs
13. Mustard Seeds — 1 tsp
14. Curry Leaves — 2 sprigs
15. Coconut Milk — 3 cups
16. Rice Flour — 1 Tbs

Salt to taste

PREPARATION:

Heat butter over high heat and add mustard to pop. Stir in the thinly chopped onions, ginger, garlic and green chili. Sauté till onions turn golden brown. Add curry leaves. Reduce heat to a minimum and add ingredients 6-10. Sauté for 1 minute. Sprinkle the rice flour over, stir and add chicken. Pour 3 cups of coconut milk, salt and cook chicken till tender for about 20 minutes. Pour in the remaining milk and stir well. Remove from heat before boiling.

MEAT

CHICKEN BREAST DELICIOUS

1. Chicken Breasts   3 lbs
2. Chili Powder   2 tsp
3. Coriander Powder   2 tsp
4. Fennel Seed Powder   1 tsp
5. Garlic Paste   1 tsp
6. Butter   3 Tbs
7. Onion   2 medium thinly sliced
   Salt to taste

PREPARATION:

Discard the skin and cut the meat into chunky pieces. Smear the meat with items 2-5. Add salt. Cook for 5 minutes over medium temperature. Heat butter and sauté onions till they turn light brown. Add chicken pieces and fry both sides till golden brown.

Extra Recipe:

THANDOORI CHICKEN

1. Chicken Legs — 4 lbs thighs & legs
2. Chili Powder — 1 Tbs
3. Hot Chili Powder — ½ tsp
4. Onion — ½ cup
5. Ginger Root — 2" long
6. Garlic — 2 Tbs
7. Coriander Leaves — 2 sprigs
8. Tomato Paste — 3 tsp
9. Yogurt — 1 ½ cup
    Salt to taste

PREPARATION:

Grind items 4-7 into a puree in a blender. Mix with chili powder (both), tomato paste, yogurt and salt. Wash and dry the chicken portions. Make a few slits on the chicken and rub the marinade all over. Set aside for an hour. Arrange them in a baking dish and bake in a hot oven for 45 to 50 minutes at 375^0 F. Check the tenderness of the chicken and serve.

CRISPY BAKED CHICKEN LEGS

1. Chicken Legs   3 lbs
2. Black Pepper   1 Tbs
3. Lemon Juice   2 Tbs
4. Eggs   2
5. Bread Crumbs   2 cups
   Salt to taste

PREPARATION:

Separate legs and thighs, wash and dry. Rub the chicken portions with lemon juice and salt. Coat with black pepper. Set aside for ½ an hour. Beat eggs together with 2 Tbs water and dip each chicken portion in the egg and roll in bread crumbs. Do this twice. Let them be thickly coated. Bake in a preheated oven for 45-minutes at 375^0 F.

MEAT

RAISIN CHICKEN

These are wonderful and your children would love it.

1. Chicken Legs — 2 lbs
2. Vinegar — 2 Tbs
3. Sugar — 4 tsp
4. Soy Sauce — 2 Tbs
5. Garlic — 4 cloves, peeled
6. Cinnamon — 1 stick 2 " long
7. Cloves — 5 whole ones
8. Raisins — ½ cup
9. Chili Powder — 1 tsp
10. Onion — 1 cubed
    Salt to taste

PREPARATION:

Combine sugar and vinegar. Arrange chicken in a baking dish. Pour the mixture over. Add soy sauce. In 1 cup water, make a fine paste of raisins in blender. Add. Mix with spices. Leave for 30 minutes. Put in cubed onion and whole garlic. Bake for 40-50 minutes at 400 F.

MEAT

MANGO CHICKEN (SWEET AND SOUR CHICKEN)

1. Chicken — 2 lbs cut to 2" pieces
2. Ripe Mango — 1 large, peel, cut
3. Butter Milk — 1 cup
4. Cinnamon — 1 stick 2" long piece
5. Cloves — 6 whole ones
6. Green Pepper — 2 cut to wedges
7. Green Chili Pepper — 1 chopped
8. Onion — 1 large, cut into cubes
9. Garlic — 3 cloves crushed
10. Mango Powder — 4 tsp
11. Yogurt — ½ cup
12. Oil or Butter — 3 Tbs

Salt to taste

PREPARATION:

Cut chicken to 2" pieces. Add the chopped green chili and mango powder. Sprinkle with salt. Pour in butter milk. Cook over medium heat till chicken is tender for about 15 to 20 minutes. Remove from heat. Sauté shallots or onion, green pepper, garlic, cinnamon, and cloves in butter for 2 minutes and pour into the chicken. Peel and cube mango. Add to the pot along with yogurt. Bring to a boil and simmer for 4-5 minutes. Serve hot with chappathi or palappam.

MEAT

BUTTER CHICKEN

This is a recipe handed down from a friend of mine. Butter chicken is a North Indian dish. However it is a favorite recipe for all.

Chicken marinade
1. Chicken
   (Boneless & skinless) 1 lb
2. Garlic Paste — 1 tsp
3. Ginger Paste — 1 tsp
4. Chili Powder — ½ tsp
5. Turmeric — ½ tsp
6. Garam Masala — 1 tsp
7. Yogurt — ½ cup
8. Lemon Juice — 1 Tbs
9. Salt — ½ tsp

To make the Sauce
1. Onion — 1 (medium) sliced
2. Ginger & Garlic paste — 1 tsp each
3. Coriander Powder — 1 Tbs
4. Chili Powder — 1 tsp
5. Cumin powder — 1 tsp
6. Tomato paste — 1 tsp
7. Tomatoes — 3 cut into cubes
8. Cinnamon — ½ tsp
9. Cloves — ¼ tsp
10. Fennel — ½ tsp
11. Turmeric — ½ tsp
12. Whipping cream — 1 cup
13. Fenugreek leaves — 1 tsp dried or fresh
14. Butter — 2 Tbs
    Salt to taste

MEAT

PREPARATION:

Combine items 2-9. Add the chicken pieces and marinate for 2 – 4 hours. Set aside. Make the sauce by heating 1 Tbs butter in a heavy bottomed pot. Add onion. Stir fry for 2 minutes till soft. Add ginger and garlic paste. Stir-fry for a minute. Reduce heat and add the items 3-11. Stir fry in medium heat for 2 minutes till the tomatoes are soft and cooked. Keep it aside. When cool, puree them in a blender with ¼ cup water. Heat 1 Tbs butter in a frying pan and add the marinated chicken and stir fry for 5-7 minutes stirring till the chicken is soft and cooked. Add the pureed sauce and boil everything for 2 minutes. Season with salt. Check the doneness of the chicken. Once it is cooked add whipping cream and simmer. Add the fenugreek leaves and serve hot with rice or chappathi.

Instead of the whipping cream use almond milk. Or blend ½ cup almonds in 1 cup water and use.

MEAT

FRIED DUCK

1. Duck — 4 lbs cut into big pieces
2. Onion — 3 sliced lengthwise thin
3. Chili powder — 1 Tbs
4. Hot Chili Powder — 1 tsp
5. Cloves — 1 tsp
6. Cinnamon — 1 tsp
7. Fennel Seed Powder — 1 ½ tsp
8. Tomato Paste — 3 tsp
   or
   Tomatoes — 4 medium (cut into four)
9. Lemon Juice — 1 Tbs
10. Oil — ½-1 cup
    Salt to taste

PREPARATION:

Cut duck into neat pieces and put into a thick bottomed pot. Add lemon juice, salt, both chili powders, tomato paste, ½ tsp cloves, ½ tsp cinnamon and 1 tsp fennel seed powder. Mix well. Add ½ cup of milk and ½ cup of water. Cover pot and cook over medium heat for 20 minutes. Cook till all water is absorbed. Remove from heat. In a skillet pour ½ cup oil and sauté sliced onion till light brown. Add duck pieces, remaining spices and stir fry both sides till all turn reddish brown.

MEAT

FAVOURITE DUCK FRY

1.	Duck	3 lbs cut into big portions
2.	Mustard Paste	1 Tbs
3.	Chili Powder	2 tsp
4.	Hot Chili Powder	½ tsp
5.	Garlic Paste	1 tsp
6.	Vinegar	1 Tbs
7.	Ginger Root	1" long chopped
8.	Shallots or Onion	1 cup thinly sliced
9.	Fennel Seed	1 tsp
10.	White Flour	1 cup
11.	Rice Flour	1 cup
12.	Oil	1 cup
	Salt to taste	

PREPARATION:

Cut the duck into big pieces and rub the meat with mustard paste, garlic paste and vinegar. Add ½ cup of water and salt and cook over medium heat for 20 minutes. Pour in 1¼ cup of water in a pot and make a thick batter by mixing the flours. Stir in chopped onion and ginger. Season with salt and fennel seeds. Heat 1 cup of oil in a skillet over high heat and when it is hot, take duck pieces one by one, soak in batter and deep fry both sides till golden brown.

MEAT

DUCK ROAST

1. Duck — 4 lbs
2. Shallots — 5 peel outer skin
3. Onion — 2 sliced thinly
4. Green Chili Pepper — 3 chopped
5. Ginger Root — 2" long grated
6. Garlic — 7 cloves crushed
7. Potatoes — 2 cooked, mashed
8. Coriander Powder — 3 tsp
9. Chili Powder — 1 tsp
10. Cloves Powder — ½ tsp
11. Cinnamon Powder — ½ tsp
12. White Flour — 1 Tbs
13. Butter — ¼ cup
14. Oil — ½ cup
15. Coconut Milk — 2 cups

Salt to taste

PREPARATION:

In a skillet pour in ½ cup oil and heat. Add sliced onion and stir fry for 3 minutes. Continue stirring and add grated ginger, garlic, and green pepper and sauté for further 2 minutes. Mix chili powder, 2 tsp coriander powder, and ¼ tsp cloves and ¼ tsp cinnamon and stir into the skillet. Reduce heat and simmer for a few seconds. Turn off heat. Combine this with mashed potatoes and salt. Take a whole duck and stuff the inside with this filling and sew it up. Make slits here and there on the duck and put it in a baking dish. Pour 2 cups of milk, whole shallots, and salt and bake it for 1½ hours at 350° F. After each half hour turn duck

MEAT

from side to side to get all sides cooked. Put ¼ cup butter in a skillet, heat and fry the duck for 5 minutes turning it from side to side. Take out and put on a plate. Add 1 Tbs white flour, and remaining spices in the remaining heated butter and stir for 5 seconds. Pour sauce and shallots. Boil and serve hot along with roasted duck.

MEAT

DUCK POTATO STEW

1. Duck — 3 lbs cut into 2" pieces
2. Potato — 4 peel, cut in to halves
3. Onion — 2 sliced thinly
4. Ginger Root — 1" piece grated
5. Garlic — 5 cloves crushed
6. Green pepper — 2 cut into four
7. Green Chili Pepper — 2 chopped
8. Cloves Powder — ½ tsp
9. Cinnamon Powder — ½ tsp
10. Fennel Seed Powder — 1 tsp
11. Cumin Seed Powder — ½ tsp
12. Turmeric — ½ tsp
13. Cardamom — ½ tsp
14. Star Anise — ½ tsp
15. Tomato — 4 medium
16. Milk — 2 cups
17. Cream — 1 cup
18. Curry Leaves — 6
19. Butter or Oil — ½ cup

Salt according to taste.

PREPARATION:

Grind ingredients 4-15 in a blender. In a heavy bottomed pot smear duck pieces with the ground paste. Heat butter or oil and fry the duck portions turning frequently for 5 minutes. Put aside. Add sliced onion in the remaining oil and sauté till golden brown. Drain and set aside. Add 1 cup of milk, 1 cup of water, and salt to the meat. Bring to a boil and add the halved potatoes and cook for 20 minutes. Pour in the

MEAT

remaining milk. Simmer for 5 minutes. Add the cream, heat well and serve immediately. Garnish the top with fried onions.

TURKEY TIT BIT

1. Turkey — 3 lbs cut into 2" portions
2. Shallot Paste — 3 tsp
3. Mustard Paste — 2 tsp
4. Garlic Paste — 3 tsp
5. Ginger Root Paste — 2 Tbs
6. Lemon Juice — 3 Tbs
7. Star Anise — 1 whole
8. Green Chili Pepper — 2 deseeded, chopped
9. Black Pepper — 1 tsp
10. Turmeric — ½ tsp
11. All Purpose Flour — ½ cup
12. Rice Flour — ½ cup
13. Cream of Wheat — 1 Tbs
    Salt to taste
    Oil for frying

PREPARATION:

Cut turkey to 2" pieces. Blend items 2 to 10 along with 1 cup water in a blender. Smear turkey with the mixture. Season with salt. Cover and bring to a boil. Cook for 20 minutes and let all the liquid be absorbed. Make a batter with all the flours in 1½ cup water. Season with salt. Soak each turkey piece in the batter and deep fry both sides till golden brown.

MEAT

SPICY TURKEY

1.	Turkey	3 lbs
2.	Cinnamon Powder	½ tsp
3.	Cloves Powder	½ tsp
4.	Fennel Seed Powder	½ tsp
5.	Fenugreek Powder	¼ tsp
6.	Garlic	10 cloves crushed
7.	Coriander Powder	2 Tbs
8.	Chili powder	2 tsp
9.	Curry Leaves	10
10.	Mustard Paste	1 Tbs
11.	Turmeric	1 tsp
12.	Tamarind	1 tsp
13.	Butter	½ cup
14.	Onion	1 chopped
15.	Coconut	1 cup grated
	Salt to taste	

PREPARATION:

Cut turkey to 2" pieces and marinate in mustard paste, turmeric and salt. Heat ¼ cup butter in a skillet or non-stick frying pan and fry the turkey both sides for about 4-5 minutes. Drain. Heat the remaining butter and sauté onion for 3 minutes. Add ingredients 2-9. Stir fry for 1 minute over low heat. Soak tamarind in 2 cups water and pour the juice into the skillet. Pour the mixture over the fried turkey. Cover and cook for 20 minutes. Make a fine paste of coconut in 1 cup water and pour in. As it boils remove from heat.

MEAT

MEAT CUTLET

1. Ground Beef — 2 cups, cooked
2. Potato — 1 cup, mashed
3. Onion — 1 chopped
4. Ginger Root — 1 Tbs, grated
5. Black Pepper — ½ tsp
6. Cloves Powder — ½ tsp
7. Bread Crumbs — 2-3 cups
8. Egg — 1-2
9. Vinegar — 2 tsp
10. Curry Leaves — 5 chopped
11. Coriander Leaves — ¼ cup chopped

Oil for frying
Salt to taste

PREPARATION:

Cook and drain all fat from meat. Cook and mash potatoes. Sauté chopped onion in 2 Tbs oil till transparent. Add grated ginger and curry leaves. Stir fry for a few seconds. Reduce heat. Add black pepper, and cloves powder. Add meat, vinegar, and salt. Stir fry. Bring in the mashed potatoes. Combine well. Remove from heat. Add ½ cup bread crumbs, coriander leaves, and egg yolk. Mix. Adjust seasoning. Make lime-size balls and flatten to oval shape. Dip in egg white and coat with bread crumbs. Deep fry both sides till golden brown. Serve with tomato salad or ketchup.

> Add 2 green chili pepper chopped to get a strong, hot flavour. Any type of ground meat can be used to make cutlets.

MEAT

MEAT

CHILI BEEF FRY

1. Stewing Beef — 3 lbs cut into 1" cubes
2. Chili Powder — 2 Tbs
3. Turmeric — 1 tsp
4. Onion — 2 cut into wedges
5. Shallot — ½ cup
6. Star Anise — 1 whole star
7. Garlic — 10 cloves
8. Tomato — 4 chopped
9. Soy Sauce — 2 Tbs
10. Oil for frying — ½ cup
    Salt to taste

PREPARATION:

Grind shallot, chili powder, star anise, turmeric and garlic into a fine paste. Mix with soy sauce and salt. Marinate meat for an hour in the mixture. Cover and cook over medium heat till all water evaporates. Heat oil and fry the meat until golden brown. In the remaining oil fry onion till crisp and golden. Drain. Add tomato pieces to the pot and stir fry for 1 minute or till they are soft. Pour it over the fried meat and stir well. Sprinkle fried onion on top and serve.

MEAT

CHILI GINGER BEEF CURRY

1. Stewing Beef — 4 lbs cut 1" pieces
2. Onion — 2
3. Ginger Root — 2" long
4. Green Chili — 2
5. Cloves Powder — ½ tsp
6. Cinnamon Powder — ½ tsp
7. Star Anise powder — ½ tsp
8. Fennel Seed — 1 tsp
9. Mint Leaves — 1 cup
10. Coriander Leaves — 1 cup
11. Chili Powder — 2 tsp
12. Turmeric — 1 tsp
13. Tomato Sauce — ½ cup
14. Chili Sauce — ¼ cup
15. Cashews — ½ cup
16. Vegetable Oil — ½ cup
    Salt to taste

PREPARATION:

Blend ingredients 2-12 into a puree. Heat butter and add puree, and sauté for 5 minutes over medium heat. Stir in meat and stir fry for 4 minutes. Season with salt and add ½ cup water. Cover and cook for 20 minutes. Stir occasionally to prevent sticking. Add the two sauces. Grind cashews to a fine paste in the blender and add. Combine well, bring to a boil and serve hot.

MEAT

SPICY BEEF FRY

1. Stewing Beef   2 lbs cut into 1" cubes
2. Onion   2 medium
3. Ginger Root   1" long
4. Garlic   4 cloves
5. Cloves   ½ tsp
6. Cinnamon Powder   ½ tsp
7. Fennel Seed Powder 1 tsp
8. Turmeric Powder   ½ tsp
9. Coriander Powder   1 Tbs
10. Chili Powder   1 Tbs
11. Hot Chili Powder   ½ tsp
12. Tomato Paste   2 tsp
13. Oil   ½ cup
    Salt to taste

PREPARATION:

Make a paste with ingredients 3-11. Smear meat with the paste, season with salt. Pour ½ cup water and cook on a medium heat. Let all water evaporate. Heat oil in a skillet and sauté onion till soft. Add cooked meat and fry all together till they become brown.

MEAT

LIVER FRY

1. Liver — 1 lb cut bite-size pieces
2. Potato — 2 cut 2" long pieces
3. Chili Powder — 2 tsp
4. Cloves Powder — ½ tsp
5. Fennel Seed Powder — 1 tsp
6. Black Pepper — 1 tsp
7. Onion — 1 thinly chopped
8. Butter — 2 Tbs
9. Vinegar — 2 tsp
   Salt to taste

PREPARATION:

Cut liver into small bite-size pieces. Mix with the potatoes. Add the spices, ¼ cup water, and salt. Cover and cook for 8 minutes. Sauté onion in butter and put the cooked liver and potatoes and stir fry for 5-7 minute over medium heat till reddish brown.

MEAT

EASY MEAT DISH

1. Stewing Beef   1 lb
2. Shallots   4 sliced
3. Chili Powder   1 tsp
4. Onion   1 medium cut lengthwise
5. Cloves Powder   ½ tsp
6. Butter   3 Tbs

PREPARATION:

Cut meat into small pieces, cook with ½ cup water and salt for 20 minutes. Shred the meat in a food processor when cool. Heat butter in a skillet and sauté onion and shallots for 2 minutes. Add minced beef and other ingredients. Stir fry till all become brown and crisp.

MEAT

MEAT

KERALA BEEF

1. Stewing Beef   2 lbs cut into cubes
2. Chili Powder   1 Tbs
3. Coriander Powder   2 tsp
4. Ginger Root   1" long grated
5. Garlic   3 crushed
6. Cinnamon Powder   ½ tsp
7. Cloves Powder   ¼ tsp
8. Cardamom Powder   ½ tsp
9. Fennel Seed Powder   ½ tsp
10. Turmeric Powder   ½ tsp
11. Curry Leaves   6
12. Coconut   ¼ cup thinly sliced
13. Onion   1 large sliced thinly
14. Vinegar   1 tsp
15. Oil   ¼ cup
    Salt to taste

PREPARATION:

In two tsp oil fry coconut to golden brown and set aside. Mix ingredients 2-10 and smear meat. Add vinegar and salt. Add ½ cup water, fried coconut and cook for ½ an hour over medium heat. In a skillet heat butter or oil, sauté onion and curry leaves. Add in the cooked meat and stir fry for 4 minutes. Serve hot.

FRIED BEEF

1. Stewing Beef — 2 lbs (bite-size pieces)
2. Onion — 1 chopped
3. Chili Powder — 1 Tbs
4. Turmeric — ½ tsp
5. Cloves Powder — ½ tsp
6. Fennel Seed Powder — 1 tsp
7. Ginger — 1 Tbs (grated)
8. Garlic — 1 Tbs (chopped)
9. Curry Leaves — 10
10. Lemon Juice — 2 tsp
11. Coconut — 3 Tbs
12. Oil — ¼ cup

Salt to taste

PREPARATION:

Heat 2 tsp oil or butter in a heavy bottomed pot and fry coconut (thinly cut) till golden brown. Add the remaining oil, chopped onion and sauté for 2 minutes. Stir in grated ginger and garlic and sauté for further 2 minutes. Put all the spices and curry leaves. Stir for a minute. Add the meat pieces, salt, lemon juice, and ½ cup water. Cook over medium heat for 20 minutes stirring occasionally.

MEAT

HAMBURGER MEAT FRY

1. Ground Beef   1 lb
2. Onion   1 sliced thinly
3. Chili Powder   1 ½ tsp
4. Green Pepper   2 cut into 1" long
5. Lemon Juice   1 tsp
6. Vegetable oil   2 Tbs

PREPARATION:

Cook ground beef on medium heat. Drain all fat. Heat 2 Tbs butter in a skillet and sauté onion and green chili for 2 minutes or till soft. Reduce heat and add chili powder. Stir in the drained meat, salt and lemon juice. Stir fry for 5 minutes or until they turn brown and crisp. Garnish with coriander leaves.

Extra Recipe:

MEAT

MEAT VEGETABLE STEW

1.	Stewing Beef	2 lbs cut into 2" cubes
2.	Onion	2 chopped
3.	Ginger Root	1" piece chopped
4.	Garlic	5 cloves chopped
5.	Green Chili	3 chopped
6.	Green Chili Pepper	2 deseeded, chopped
7.	Coriander Powder	½ tsp
8.	Black Pepper	½ tsp
9.	Cloves Powder	½ tsp
10.	Cinnamon	2" long ground or whole
11.	White Flour	2 Tbs
12.	Potato, Carrot	½ cup each
13.	Green Peas, Celery	½ cup each
14.	Vinegar	1 Tbs
15.	Oil	4 Tbs
	Salt to taste	

PREPARATION:

Heat oil in a heavy bottomed pot and sauté sliced onions. When onions become soft add chopped ginger, garlic, chili pepper and green chili and stir-fry for 3 minutes. Reduce heat and add all spices (items 7-10). Simmer for 2 minutes. Add the meat and stir well. Season with salt. Pour 1 cup of hot water and cook meat for 20 minutes. Add vegetables, vinegar and sugar. Adjust seasoning. Simmer over medium heat for 7 minutes. Mix the flour in ¼ cup water and pour into meat and vegetables. Stir well. When sauce is thickened remove from heat.

MEAT

RED MEAT CURRY

1. Stewing Beef — 2 lbs
2. Potato — 2 peeled, halved
3. Chili Powder — 1 Tbs
4. Fennel Seed Powder — 1 tsp
5. Cloves Powder — ½ tsp
6. Poppy Seed — ½ tsp
7. Ginger Root — 1" piece
8. Garlic — 3 cloves
9. Turmeric — ½ tsp
9. Curry Leaves — 8
10. Shredded coconut — ½ cup
    or
    Coconut Milk — 1 cup
11. Shallots — 5
12. Butter — 2 Tbs
    Salt to taste

PREPARATION:

Make a paste of chili powder, fennel seed powder, cloves, shallots, ginger, garlic, turmeric, and poppy seed in a blender. Combine it with tomato paste and salt. Marinate meat in it. Cover and cook meat over medium heat for 20 minutes. Heat butter in another pot and fry onion to golden brown, add curry leaves and sauté for a minute. Add cooked meat to the pot along with the sauce and stir well. Make a fine paste of the coconut in ½ cup water and pour into the meat. Heat well. Do not boil. Instead of coconut, 1 cup coconut milk can be added.

MEAT

Extra Recipe:

MEAT

LAMB ROAST

1.	Stewing Lamb	2 lbs cut into 1" cubes
2.	Onion	1 slice thinly
3.	Ginger Root	1" long
4.	Garlic	4 cloves
5.	Turmeric	½ tsp
6.	Chili Powder	1 tsp
7.	Star Anise	1 tsp
8.	Fennel Seed	½ tsp
9.	Cloves	4
10.	Shredded Coconut	½ cup
11.	Lemon Juice	1 Tbs
12.	Butter	4 Tbs
	Salt to taste	

PREPARATION:

Season meat with salt and lemon juice and cook for 20 minutes over medium heat in ½ cup water. Turn the meat occasionally to avoid sticking. Meanwhile in a frying pan, dry fry the coconut, star anise, fennel seed, and cloves for 3 minutes stirring constantly. Remove from heat and make a fine paste in a blender by adding ½ cup water. Add grated ginger, crushed garlic, chili powder and turmeric to the cooked meat. Stir in the coconut paste. Combine and bring to a boil. Simmer for 5 minutes. In a skillet heat 4 Tbs butter and sauté onion till golden brown. Add the meat and stir fry for 3 minutes. Serve hot.

MEAT

LAMB BROWNIE

1. Lamb Meat — 2 lbs boneless
2. Shallots (onion) — ½ cup chopped
3. Ginger Root — 1" piece grated
4. Garlic — 6 cloves crushed
5. Green Chili Pepper — 2 chopped, deseeded
6. Black Pepper — ½ Tbs
7. Allspice — ½ tsp
8. Coriander Powder — ½ tsp
9. Red Chili powder — ½ tsp
10. Vegetable Oil — ¼ cup

Salt to taste

PREPARATION:

Cut meat as thin as possible. Tenderise the meat with a meat mallet. Marinate the meat with onion, ginger, garlic, green chili, black pepper and red chili for 3 hours. Even it is better to keep overnight. Heat oil in a skillet or non-stick frying pan and put in the marinated meat. Bring to a boil. Cover and cook over medium heat till meat becomes tender and all water is evaporated. Add allspice and coriander and stir fry till meat turns brown about 5 minutes.

MEAT

BRAIN ROAST

1. Brain (Cow or Lamb) 1
2. Black Pepper   ½ tsp
3. Lemon Juice   ½ tsp
4. Egg   1
5. All Purpose Flour   ½ cup
6. Butter   2 Tbs
   Salt to taste

PREPARATION:

Clean and wash brain in salt water. Pour in ¼ cup water and cook for 7-10 minutes. When all the liquid is absorbed turn off heat. Cut it into thin slices when it is cool. Mix black pepper, vinegar, and salt and coat brain slices. Make a batter with flour, ¼ cup water, egg yolk and 2 Tbs melted butter. Pour in egg white beaten stiff. Mix lightly and dip the brain slices one by one and deep fry turning both sides.

MEAT

PORK VINDALOO

Savory & exotic

1. Pork — 2 lbs cut 1" cubes
2. Chili powder — 2 tsp
3. Hot Chili Powder — ½ tsp
4. Fenugreek Powder — ½ tsp
3. Mustard Seeds — 1 tsp
4. Onion — 2 sliced thin
5. Garlic — 5 cloves
6. Turmeric — ½ tsp
7. Tomato paste — 3 tsp
8. Vinegar — 1 Tbs
9. Sugar — ½ tsp
10. Butter — 3 Tbs
    Salt to taste

PREPARATION:

Heat butter in a heavy bottomed pot. Add thinly sliced onion and sauté for 5 minutes or till light brown. Add crushed garlic. Sauté for a few seconds and add ground fenugreek and mustard. Stir in tomato paste and reduce heat to a minimum. Simmer for 3 minutes. Add turmeric and both chili powder. Increase heat and then add meat. Pour in vinegar, salt and ½ cup water and cook for 20 minutes or till the meat is tender. Before removing from heat add sugar and allow the sauce to thicken.

Serve hot with Spaghetti, rice or corn.

MEAT

PORK FRY

1. Pork — 2 lbs cut into 1" cubes
2. Chili Powder — 2 tsp
3. Coriander Powder — 1 tsp
4. Turmeric Powder — ½ tsp
5. Tomato — 3 cut into 4
6. Onion — 2 cut lengthwise
7. Cinnamon Powder — ½ tsp
8. Cloves — ¾ tsp
9. Fennel Seed Powder — 1 tsp
10. Ginger Root — 1 Tbs (minced)
11. Garlic — 1 Tbs (minced)
12. Oil — ½ cup

PREPARATION:

Cut meat into 1" pieces. Mix or blend ingredients 2-9 and smear the meat with it. Add ½ cup water and cook the meat for 20 minutes till all water is absorbed. In a frying pan melt butter and sauté onion till soft and light brown. Add chopped ginger and garlic and stir for 1 minute. Add the meat and stir fry till all turn crisp and brown.

EGGS & RICE

EGGS

EGG MASALA ROAST

1. Eggs — 6
2. Ginger Root — ½ " piece chopped
3. Onion — 2 sliced lengthwise
4. Tomatoes — 4 chopped
5. Coriander Powder — 2 tsp
6. Chili Powder — ½ tsp
7. Black Pepper — 1 tsp
8. Turmeric — ¼ tsp
9. Cloves Powder — ¼ tsp
10. Cinnamon Powder — ¼ tsp
11. Fennel Seed Powder — ½ tsp
12. Curry Leaves — 10
13. Mustard Seeds — ½ tsp
14. Butter or Margarine — 4 Tbs

Salt to taste

PREPARATION:

Place eggs in a saucepan of cold water. Bring to a boil and simmer for 3 minutes. Shell eggs and make small slits all over. Cut onion thinly and grate ginger. Melt butter in a skillet, pop up mustard. Sauté onion and ginger for 3 minutes. Add tomatoes and sauté for another 2 minutes over low heat. Combine rest of the ingredients and add to the simmering pot. Stir-fry for 1 minute. Add salt and eggs. Roast eggs over low heat by stirring constantly for 2-3 minutes. Add 4 table spoon water and stir, fry the egg masala till all liquid is evaporated and the sauce well coated over the eggs. Serve with corn, rice or bread.

EGG CARROT DISH

1. Eggs — 2
2. Onion — ½ cup chopped
3. Black Pepper — ½ tsp
4. Carrot (grated) — 1 cup
5. Lemon Juice — ½ tsp
6. Butter — 2 Tbs
   Salt to taste

PREPARATION:

Melt butter and sauté onion till golden brown. Remove from heat. Whisk eggs. Add grated carrots, salt pepper and sautéed onion. Combine. Heat butter in a non-stick pan and pour in the carrot mixture. Cover and cook for a few seconds on medium heat. When one side is cooked turn over. Cook further for a few seconds.

EGG COCONUT DISH

1. Eggs   4
2. Coconut   1 cup grated
3. Onion   ½ cup chopped
4. Green Chili Pepper   1 chopped
5. Ginger Root   ¼ " piece grated
6. Butter   1-2 Tbs
   Salt to taste

PREPARATION:

Beat eggs well and add grated coconut and salt and combine. Sauté onion, ginger and chili pepper in 2 tsp butter for 1 minute and add to eggs. Mix the batter. Melt the remaining butter in a frying pan and pour in the egg mixture and spread like a small pancake. Reduce heat. Cover and cook gently till it is lightly set. Turn over and cook for further 1-2 minutes. Serve hot with rice or toast.

TASTY EGG PATTIES

1. Eggs — 5
2. Onion — ½ cup
3. Ginger Root — ¼" piece
4. Chili Powder — ¼ tsp
5. Coconut — 1 cup grated
6. Butter — 1 Tbs
7. Curry Leaves — 5
   Salt to taste

PREPARATION:

In a frying pan fry chili powder for 2 seconds over medium heat. Blend coconut, ginger, onion and chili powder into a puree. Beat eggs together and combine with coconut mixture. Season with salt and curry leaves. In a griddle or non-stick frying pan heat butter. When it is hot pour half of batter and spread like a small pancake. Cover and cook over low heat for 1 minute till it is lightly set. Turn over gently. When both sides are cooked take out and place on a serving plate. Make similar egg patties. Serve with rice or bread.

PRAWNS AND EGG

1. Prawns — 1 cup
2. Eggs — 4
3. Ginger Root — 1/8" piece grated
4. Onion or Shallots — ½ cup chopped
4. Black Pepper — ½ tsp
5. Vinegar — 1 tsp
6. Sugar — 3/4 tsp
7. Butter or Oil — 3 Tbs
   Salt to taste

PREPARATION:

Cook prawns in ¼ cup water, salt, vinegar and sugar for 5-8 minutes. Heat 1 table spoon butter in a frying pan and sauté onion over medium heat for 2 minutes or till soft. Add cooked prawns and stir-fry for 2 minutes. Remove from heat. Beat eggs well and season with salt, black pepper and grated ginger. In a griddle or frying pan melt 1 table spoon butter and when hot, pour in half of beaten egg and make a thin pancake. Cover and cook for a few seconds. When it is cooked place half of the filling (prawns) in the centre. Turn both sides towards centre covering the filling. Transfer it gently to a plate and make the remaining ones.

EGGS & RICE

RICE

CHICKEN BIRIYANI

1. Chicken — 4 lbs
2. Onion — 2 cut thin lengthwise
3. Ginger Root — 2 Tbs grated
4. Garlic — 8 cloves
5. Green Chili Pepper — 2(medium), chopped
6. Curry leaves — 10
7. Cloves Powder — ½ tsp
8. Cinnamon — ½ tsp
9. Fennel Seed Powder — 1 tsp
10. Coriander Powder — 1 Tbs
10. Cardamom Powder — ½ tsp
12. Turmeric Powder — ½ tsp
11. Black Pepper — ½ tsp
12. Yogurt — 1 cup
13. Rice (Basmati) — 3 cups
14. Butter or Margarine — ½ cup
15. Vegetable Oil — ¼ cup
16. Cashews & raisins — ½ cup
17. Eggs — 4

Salt to taste

PREPARATION:

In a heavy bottomed pot heat 1 Tbs butter. Fry cashews and raisins and set aside. Pour in vegetable oil. Sauté 1 cup onion till light brown. Stir in chili pepper and curry leaves. Make a puree of remaining onion, ginger, and garlic. Add puree and stir fry for 5 minutes. Add remaining spices. Stir well and add chicken pieces. Pour in yogurt and salt. Cover and cook for 20 minutes or till chicken is cooked. Remove from heat with 1 cup sauce.

Wash and cook rice in 4 cups of water with turmeric and salt till rice becomes tender. In a wok heat ½ cup butter with 2 cardamom pods and stir fry the cooked rice for 3-5 minutes. In a serving plate spread one layer of rice and top it with chicken and gravy. Hard boil eggs and remove shell. Decorate top with fried onion, cashews, eggs, and raisins.

CHICKEN BIRIYANI 2

1. Chicken — 4 lbs
2. Onion — 2 cut thin lengthwise
3. Ginger Root — 2" piece grated
4. Garlic — 8 cloves chopped
5. Green Chili Pepper — 2 deseeded, chopped
6. Cloves Powder — ½ tsp
7. Cinnamon — ½ tsp
8. Fennel Seed Powder — 1 tsp
9. Yogurt — 1 cup
10. Butter or Margarine — 3 Tbs
11. Coriander leaves — 3 Tbs chopped

Salt according to taste

PREPARATION:

Discard skin and cut chicken to neat pieces. In a heavy bottomed pot heat butter and sauté onion, ginger, chili pepper and garlic. When they become soft add half of coriander leaves, cloves, cinnamon, and fennel seed. Stir well for 10 seconds and add chicken pieces. Pour in yogurt, salt, and ¼ cup water. Cover and cook for 20 to 30 minutes or till chicken is cooked. Remove from heat with 1 cup sauce.

EGGS & RICE

RICE
1. Rice — 2 cups
2. Butter — ½ cup
3. Cardamom — 3 pods
4. Star Anise — ½ of one star
5. Cinnamon — 1" long piece
6. Rosewater — 1 tsp
7. Turmeric — ½ tsp
8. Onion — 2 cut to thin strips
9. Oil — ½ cup (for frying)
10. Cashews & Raisins — ¼ cup each
11. Eggs — 5
    Salt to taste

PREPARATION:

Wash and soak rice in water for ½ an hour. Drain off water. In ½ cup oil fry onions till golden brown and set aside. Fry cashews and raisins in 2 table spoon butter. Heat ½ cup butter, add cardamom, star anise and cinnamon and sauté for a few seconds over medium heat. Add the rice, stir-fry for 5 minutes or till rice is opaque. Add 3 cups of boiled water, Turmeric, and salt. Cover and cook rice over low heat till all water is evaporated. In a baking tray put one layer of rice and top it with one layer of chicken, rosewater, and sauce. Make one more layer similarly. Cover the top chicken pieces with a little more rice. Drop or spread fried onion, cashews and raisins over rice. Cover with foil and bake for 20 minutes at 350^0 F. Hard boil eggs in a saucepan and shell them. Serve hot biriyani in a plate with egg and coriander leaves in the middle.

EGGS & RICE

EGGS & RICE

BAKED BIRIANI

1.	Chicken	2 lbs
2.	Onion	2 cups cut into strips
3.	Star Anise	1 star
4.	Cardamom	3 pods
5.	Cloves	5 (whole ones)
6.	Fennel Seed	1 tsp
7.	Cinnamon	1" long
8.	Ginger Root	1" piece grated
9.	Garlic	4 cloves
10.	Soy Sauce	1 Tbs
11.	White Rice	2 cups
12.	Water	3 cups
13.	Butter	1/4 cup
14.	Yogurt	1 cup
15.	Oil	½ cup
16.	Cashew & Raisin	¼ cup each
	Salt to taste	

PREPARATION:

In a frying pan heat ½ cup oil and fry onion till golden brown. Drain on paper towels. Soak rice in water for ½ an hour. Drain in a colander. In another pot heat butter and sauté ginger and garlic for 5 minutes. Add cinnamon, cloves, star anise, and cardamom and stir for a few seconds. Cut chicken to 2" pieces and stir in. Stir fry for 3-5 minutes. Remove from heat and empty the contents to a baking dish. Add rice along with 3 cups boiled water, yogurt, salt and soy sauce. Add fried onion, cashews and raisins and bake in a pre-heated oven at 375^0 F for 1 hour. Check the doneness of the chicken and rice. Stir occasionally.

EGGS & RICE

Let all water evaporate. Serve hot.

Extra Recipe:

PLAIN FRIED RICE

1. White Rice — 2 cups
2. Water — 3/4 cup
3. Onion — ½ cup cut thin
4. Ginger Root — ½" piece
5. Star Anise — 1
6. Fennel Seed Powder — 1 tsp
7. Cloves Powder — ½ tsp
8. Cinnamon Powder — ½ tsp
9. Turmeric Powder — ½ tsp
10. Broken Cashews — ¼ cup
11. Raisins — ¼ cup
12. Butter — 1/2 cup

Salt to taste

PREPARATION:

Soak rice in water for 20 minutes. Drain. In a thick pot heat butter and sauté onion, ginger, and star anise for 5 minutes. Add cinnamon, cloves, turmeric and fennel seed powder. Stir for a few seconds. Pour in water. As water boils add rice. Season with salt. Stir well and reduce heat to minimum. After 13 minutes cover the lid with a damp cloth and turn off the heat. Let it remain covered for further 10 minutes. The rice will be fluffy and soft, ready to be served with any kind of curry. Before serving decorate the top with cashews and raisins fried in a little butter. Mint leaves or parsley can be used for garnishing.

EGGS & RICE

LAMB BIRIANI

1. Lamb — 2 lbs cut 1" pieces
2. Onion — 4 sliced thinly
3. Ginger Root — 1" long chopped
4. Garlic — 4 cloves
5. Green Pepper — 1 chopped
6. Green Chili Pepper — 1 chopped
7. Fennel Seed Powder — 1 tsp
8. Cloves — 6 whole ones
9. Cardamom — 3 pods
10. Cinnamon — 1" long 2 pieces
11. Black Pepper — 1 tsp
12. Coconut Milk — 2 cups
13. White Rice — 2 cups
14. Butter — ½ cup
15. Oil — ½ cup for frying
16. Mint — ¼ cup chopped
17. Coriander Leaves — ¼ cup chopped
17. Lemon Juice — 3 Tbs

Salt to taste.

PREPARATION:

Deep fry 2 onions thinly sliced in oil till golden brown. Set aside. Fry cashews and raisins and drain. In a skillet heat ½ cup butter or margarine. Sauté remaining 2 onions, ginger, garlic, green pepper, and chili pepper. When they become soft add cloves, cardamom, fennel seed powder, black pepper and cinnamon. Stir for 2 minutes. Add mint and coriander leaves chopped well. Stir for another minute. Add meat. Adjust seasoning. Pour in one cup of milk and cover and cook for 20 minutes. Dribble lemon juice.

EGGS & RICE

Add remaining 1 cup of milk and 2 cups of water. Wash and drain the rice and add in. Bake the whole mixture in a hot oven at 375^0 F till all water is absorbed and rice cooked. Stir at times. Decorate the top with fried onion and cashews.

VEGETABLE & PRAWN FRIED RICE

1. White Rice — 2 cups
2. Prawns — 2 cups
3. Beans, Carrots, Peas — 3 cups
4. Ginger root — 1" piece grated
5. Garlic — 4 cloves chopped
6. Onion — 1 thinly chopped
7. Soy Sauce — 2 Tbs
8. Cloves — 5 whole ones
9. Cardamom — 3 pods
10. Turmeric — ½ tsp
11. Eggs — 5
13. Raisins & Cashews — ¼ cup each
14. Butter — ½ cup
    Salt to taste

PREPARATION:

In 2 table spoon butter sauté onion till soft. Add grated ginger and garlic and sauté for 2 minutes. Add prawns, salt and ¼ cup water and cook prawns over medium heat till all water is evaporated. Cut carrots and beans horizontally to 1" long thin slices. In 1 table spoon butter sauté peas, carrots and beans. Add 1 table spoon soy sauce and simmer over medium heat for 2-3 minutes or till they become soft. Heat butter in a thick bottomed pot and fry cardamom and cloves for 3 seconds. Add washed and drained rice and stir-fry for 3-4 minutes. Pour in 3 cups boiled water and reduce heat to minimum. Add ½ tsp turmeric and 1 table spoon soy sauce. Season with salt. Stir well and cover till cooked. When water evaporates remove from heat. Beat the eggs lightly. Heat 2 table spoon butter in a

EGGS & RICE

frying pan and pour in the eggs stirring all the time till they are set and cooked. In a baking tray spread one layer of rice and top it with one layer of prawns followed by a layer of vegetables. Fry cashews and raisins in butter and decorate the top. Cover with a foil and place in the oven. Just before serving bake it for 15 minutes at 375^0 F.

SIMPLE FRIED RICE

1. Basmati Rice   2 cups
2. Cinnamon   2 pieces 1" long
3. Cloves   5 whole ones
4. Cardamom   4 pods
5. Turmeric   ½ tsp
6. Butter   4 Tbs
7. Water   3 ½ cups
8. Cashews & Raisins   ½ cup
   Salt to taste

PREPARATION:

Place rice, water, salt and spices in a baking dish. Put butter on top. Cover with foil and bake at 400 F till all water is evaporated. Stir occasionally. Fry cashews and raisins in 1 table spoon butter, drain and garnish on top before serving.

QUICK VEGETABLE BIRIANI

1. White Rice — 2 cups
2. Vegetables — 3 cups
   (Carrots, peas,
   Beans, celery) — cut ½" diagonally
3. Cardamom — 4 pods
4. Cloves — 8 whole
5. Cinnamon — 2" long
6. Turmeric — ½ tsp
7. Soy Sauce — 2 Tbs
8. Butter — 2 Tbs
9. Onion — 1 large sliced thin
10. Cashews & Raisins — ½ cup
    Salt to taste

PREPARATION:

Heat 12 cups of water in a pot. Wash and add rice. Add turmeric, spices, and salt to the rice. Pour in soy sauce. Stir well and bring to a boil. Reduce heat to minimum. Let rice simmer for 7 more minutes. Drain. Cook diced vegetables in a small pot, with 1 table spoon butter and salt for 3-4 minutes stirring occasionally. In ½ cup oil deep fry thinly sliced onion till golden brown. Drain. In 1 tablespoon butter fry raisins and cashews. In a baking dish layer rice and vegetables. Spread the remaining rice on top. Heat 1 tablespoon butter till golden yellow and sprinkle over the rice. Garnish top with fried onions, cashews and raisins. Cover with foil and keep in oven. Just before serving bake it for 20 minutes at 375^0 F.

EGGS & RICE

CARROT RICE

1. White Rice — 2 cups
2. Onion — 1 medium
3. Coconut — 1 cup grated
4. Cumin Powder — ¼ tsp
5. Carrots — 1 ½ cup grated
6. Turmeric — ½ tsp
7. Cloves — 4
8. Cinnamon — 1" piece
9. Cardamom — 4
10. Black Pepper — ½ tsp
11. Lemon Juice — 2 Tbs
12. Eggs — 4
13. Broken Cashews — ¼ cup
14. Raisins — ¼ cup
15. Butter — ½ cup
    Salt to taste

PREPARATION:

Wash and drain the rice. Heat ¼ cup butter over high heat and fry cardamom, cloves and cinnamon for a few seconds. Add rice and stir fry for 5 minutes. Add 3 cups boiled water, salt, and turmeric. Cover and cook over low heat till rice is cooked and dry. Meanwhile in the remaining butter sauté the chopped onion till golden brown and sprinkle black pepper and cumin powder. Add coconut and stir for a minute. Mix with the grated carrots and stir fry for another minute. Add 1 table spoon lemon juice and remove from heat. Pour 1 Tbs lemon juice over the rice. In a baking dish spread one layer of rice and top with the carrots. Hard

EGGS & RICE

boil eggs, remove shells and cut into thin slices. Decorate the top with egg slices, fried nuts, and lemon wedges. Bake for 15 minutes at 375^0 F. Serve hot.

THAIRU SADHAM (YOGURT RICE)

1. Cooked Rice   4 cups
2. Yogurt   2 cups
3. Onion   ½ cup, thinly chopped
4. Ginger Root   ½" long grated
5. Green Chili Pepper   2 deseeded
6. Urad (split) Dal   ½ tsp
7. Mustard Seeds   1 tsp
8. Curry Leaves   5
9. Butter   ¼ cup
   Salt to taste

PREPARATION:

Heat butter and add mustard. When it pops, add urad. After a few seconds add onion, green chili, curry leaves, and ginger. Stir-fry till all become soft or light brown. Reduce heat. Add cooked rice. Stir fry. Remove from heat. Pour in yogurt stirring continuously. After the rice mixture cools down, add salt. Mix well and serve hot or cold with mango pickle or lemon pickle.

EGGS & RICE

LEMON RICE

1. Cooked rice   2 cups
2. Lemon   Juice of one lemon
3. Onion   ½ cup chopped
4. Green Chili Pepper 1 cut round and thin
5. Ginger Root   ¼" piece chopped
6. Garlic   2 cloves chopped
7. Mustard Seeds   1 tsp
8. Butter   2 Tbs
9. Curry Leaves   4
   Salt to taste

PREPARATION:

Add mustard seed to melted butter. When mustard pops, add chili pepper, ginger, garlic, and curry leaves. Sauté for 3 minutes. Reduce heat and add cooked rice, stir well. Sprinkle with lemon juice and salt. Mix well and serve.

EGGS & RICE

CHILI RICE

1. Cooked rice   2 cups
2. Onion   ½ cup chopped
3. Ginger Root   ¼" piece chopped
4. Mustard Seeds   1 tsp
5. Paprika   2 tsp
6. Chili Powder   ½ tsp
7. Curry leaves   5
8. Butter   2Tbs

PREPARATION:

Add mustard seed to melted butter. When mustard pops add onion, ginger, and curry leaves. Sauté for 1-2 minutes. Reduce heat, add both paprika and chilli powder. Immediately add cooked rice, stir well. Season with salt. Mix well and serve.

Extra Recipe:

SEA FOOD

SEA FOOD

FISH

FISH CUTLET

1. Fish — 2 lbs
2. Ginger Root — ½" long chopped
3. Garlic — 3 cloves chopped
4. Onion — 1 cup chopped
5. Green Chili Pepper — 2 cut chopped
6. Mint Leaves — 2 sprigs chopped
7. Eggs — 2
8. Black Pepper — ¼ tsp
9. Cloves Powder — ¼ tsp
10. Vinegar — 1 tsp
11. Bread Crumbs — 2 cups
12. Oil for frying

Salt according to taste

PREPARATION:

Cook fish with a little water and salt. Remove bones and shred with a fork. Fry onion, ginger, garlic, and green pepper in 2 tablespoon oil till light brown. Add mint leaves. Reduce heat and add black pepper and cloves. Stir in the fish. Season with vinegar and salt. Remove from heat. Separate yolks and whites of eggs and mix the yolks with fish. Add ½ cup bread crumbs. Combine well and make small lemon size balls. Flatten each ball, dip in egg white, soak with bread crumbs and deep fry both sides till brown and crisp. For best result use Salmon, or Halibut.

SEA FOOD

KERALA FISH CUTLETS

A crowd pleaser, old favourite

1. Fish — 2 lbs
2. Potato — ¾ lb cooked, mashed
3. Ginger Root — 1 Tbs grated
4. Onion — 1 chopped
5. Green Pepper — 1 chopped
6. Black Pepper — ½ tsp
7. Cloves — ½ tsp
8. Curry Leaves — 5
9. Eggs — 2
10. Bread Crumbs — 2 cups
11. Vinegar — 1 Tbs
12. Oil for frying
    Salt to taste

PREPARATION:

Peel, cook, and mash potatoes. Cook fish with a little water and salt for 5 minutes. Let all water evaporate. Take out bones and shred with a fork. In 2 tablespoons of oil sauté onion, ginger, chili, and curry leaves. Reduce heat and add black pepper and cloves powder. Add fish and stir fry for a minute. Season with vinegar and salt. Add mashed potatoes and mix thoroughly. Remove from heat. Make lime-size balls, flatten them. Dip each one in egg white and coat with bread crumbs. Deep fry on both sides till brown. Take out with a slotted spoon and drain. Serve hot with tomato sauce or chili sauce.

SEA FOOD

SEA FOOD

FRIED FISH

Excellent for a party.

1. Fish   2 lbs cut into 2" squares
   (Whole fish can be used as well)
2. Onion   2
3. Ginger Root   1 ½" long
4. Garlic   6 cloves
5. Green Chili Pepper   2
6. Vinegar   1 Tbs
7. Chili Powder   2 Tbs
8. Turmeric   ½ tsp
9. Tomato   3 finely chopped
   Oil for frying
   Salt to taste

PREPARATION:

Clean and cut fish into 2" squares or chunks. Grind or make a puree of items 2-8 in a blender. Take half of it and marinate fish pieces for 1 to 2 hours. Sauté the remaining puree in 3 tablespoon oil for 5 minutes. Add tomatoes. Cook till tomatoes become tender. Stir fry over medium heat for 1-2 minutes. Meanwhile heat oil in a frying pan over high heat and deep fry the marinated fish on both sides. Drain on paper towels. Arrange fried fish on a warmed serving dish and pour the gravy over it. Garnish with lemon slices and serve immediately.

SEA FOOD

COUNTRY STYLE FISH FRY

1. Fish — 2 lbs cut into 2" chunks
2. Onion — ½ cup
3. Ginger Root — 1" long
4. Garlic — 5 cloves
6. Turmeric — ½ tsp
7. Chili powder — 1 Tbs
8. Hot Chili Powder — ½ tsp (optional)
9. Black Pepper — 1 tsp
10. Vinegar — 1 Tbs
11. Oil for frying
    Salt to taste

PREPARATION:

Grind items 2-9 into a fine paste with a little water and vinegar. Mix with salt. Smear fish pieces with the paste and set aside for 1 to 2 hours. Heat oil in a frying pan enough to cover the fish pieces and deep fry on both sides till brown and crisp. Drain on paper towels. Serve hot.
Marinated fish can be kept in the fridge for overnight. This adds more flavour to the fish.

SEA FOOD

BAKED FISH

1. Fish — 2 lbs cut into large pieces
2. Onion — 1
3. Chili Powder — 1 Tbs
4. Black Pepper — 1 tsp
5. Ginger Root — ½" long
6. Garlic — 4 cloves
7. Lemon Juice — 1 Tbs
8. Butter — 2 Tbs
   Salt to taste

PREPARATION:

Make a paste of items 2-6 in a blender with lemon juice and salt. Marinate fish in the paste for an hour. Grease a baking dish and arrange fish in one layer. Dot the top with butter. Bake for 20 minutes at 450^0 F till fish is soft and top crisp. When both sides turn light brown take out. Garnish with coriander leaves and serve.

FISH IN COCONUT MILK

1. Fish — 2 lbs cut into 3"squares
2. Turmeric — ½ tsp
3. Chili Powder — 1 Tbs
3. Ginger Root — ½" piece
4. Garlic — 5 cloves
5. Cumin Seed Powder — ½ tsp
6. Onion — 2 cut into thin strips
7. Green Chili Pepper — 2 split the sides
8. Ginger Root — ½" piece chop
9. Coconut Milk — 2 cups
10. Lemon Juice — 1 Tbs
    or
    Tamarind — 3 pieces
11. Oil — 4 Tbs
    Salt to taste

PREPARATION:

Grind items 2-5 into a fine puree in a blender. Marinate fish for 1 hour. Stir fry onion, ginger, and green pepper in 4 tablespoon oil for 3 minutes. Put in marinated fish. Add salt and tamarind. Stir well. Pour in coconut milk. Let it be cooked over medium heat for 10-15 minutes.

SEA FOOD

STUFFED FISH

1. Fish — 2 lbs
2. Onion — 2
3. Ginger Root — 1" long
4. Garlic — 5 cloves
5. Black Pepper — ½ tsp
6. Chili Powder — 3 tsp
7. Green Pepper — 2 deseeded
8. Tomato Sauce — 1 Tbs
9. Curry Leaves — 5
10. Vegetable Oil — ½ cup
    Salt to taste

PREPARATION:

In a blender blend ingredients 2-7. Mix with tomato sauce and salt. Make slits on fish on both sides and stuff the slits and stomach with the paste. Set aside for 1 hour. Top the fish with the left over paste and curry leaves. Brush oil on both sides of the fish and bake. Bake at 450° F, till it is cooked and crisp. (20-25 min.) The fish can also be deep fried.

SEA FOOD

FISH MOLEE

Tastes real yummy

1. Fish — 2 lbs
2. Onion — 1 cut into thin strips
3. Ginger Root — 1" piece chopped
4. Garlic — 6 cloves chopped
5. Lemon Juice — 1 Tbs
6. Green Pepper — 1 chopped
7. Green Chili Pepper — 3 deseeded cut in halves
8. Coconut Milk — 2 cups
9. Corn Flour — 1 Tbs
10. Tomato — 3 cut round and thin
11. Oil — 3 Tbs

Salt to taste

PREPARATION:

Wash and cut fish into 2" squares. Heat oil in a heavy bottomed pan and sauté onion till it becomes transparent. Add ginger, garlic, and green chilies. Stir fry for 3 minutes. Reduce heat and add corn flour. Stir continuously. Add fish and squeeze in the lemon juice. Add salt and simmer for a minute. Pour 1 cup milk. Bring to a boil. Cover and cook for 4-5 minutes over medium heat. Add the remaining milk. Cook over low heat for 2 minutes. Stir occasionally to avoid sticking. Place the tomato rings on top. Simmer for 2 minutes, adjust seasoning and turn off heat. This is a very good curry to eat with any kind of bread and bun.

SEA FOOD

RED FISH CURRY (MEEN CURRY)

1. Fish — 2 lbs
2. Onion — ½ cup
3. Ginger Root — 2" long chopped
4. Garlic — 6 cloves chopped
5. Chili Powder — 2 Tbs
6. Hot Chili Powder — 1 tsp
7. Tomato Paste — 6 tsp
8. Tamarind — 3 pieces
9. Fenugreek — ½ tsp
10. Curry Leaves — 9
11. Oil — ¼ cup
   Salt to taste

PREPARATION:

Clean and cut fish into 2" long chunks. In a heavy bottomed pot sauté onion till soft. Add ginger, garlic, and curry leaves. Stir fry for 2 minutes. Stir in tomato paste, reduce heat and simmer for further 1-2 minutes. Add chili powder, turmeric, hot chili, and fenugreek powder. Sauté for a few seconds. Increase heat and pour in 2 to 2½ cups of water. Season with salt and tamarind. Bring to a boil. Add fish. Cover and cook for 10-15 minutes, the first half over medium heat and the last half over low heat. This is a good curry with rice or cassava.

SEA FOOD

FISH AND PEAS STEW

1.	Fish	2 lbs cut into 2" squares
2.	Peas	2 cups
3.	Onion	1 chop thinly
4.	Black Mustard	1 tsp
5.	Garlic	6 cloves crushed
6.	Green Chili Pepper	2 chopped
7.	Cloves	4 whole ones
8.	Vinegar	1 Tbs
9.	Tomato	3 cut round and thin
10.	Corn Flour	1 Tbs
11.	Milk	2 cups
12.	Oil	3 Tbs
	Salt to taste	

PREPARATION:

Heat oil in a wok over medium heat and add mustard to pop up. Stir in onion and cloves and sauté for a while. Add crushed garlic and green chili. Stir fry for 2 minutes. Add green peas, vinegar, and salt. Add fish gently. Simmer for a minute. Pour in 1 cup of milk and ½ cup water. Bring to a boil and cook covered for 5-8 minutes over medium heat. Dissolve corn flour in the remaining milk and pour in. When the stew boils place tomato rings on top. Simmer for 3 minutes. Serve hot with chappathi or bread.

SEA FOOD

COCONUT FISH (MEEN PEERA)

1. Fish — 1 lb cut into 1" pieces
2. Coconut — 1 cup fresh and grated
3. Onion — ½ cup chopped
4. Ginger Root — ½" long chopped
5. Garlic — 4 cloves chopped
6. Green Chili Pepper — 1 chopped
7. Cumin Seed Powder — ¼ tsp
8. Turmeric — ¼ tsp
9. Curry Leaves — 5
10. Tamarind — 2 pieces
    Salt to taste

PREPARATION:

Mix together ingredients 2-8 in a food processor or blender to a coarse paste. Cut tamarind into small pieces and place in ½ cup salted water. Clean and cut the fish into 1" pieces. Place the fish in a heavy bottomed pot and add the coconut mixture. Add tamarind and the salted water. Adjust the seasoning. Sprinkle in the curry leaves. Cook covered for 8-10 minutes over medium heat till all the water is absorbed. Goes well with rice.

SEA FOOD

FRIED FISH

Quick and tasty

1. Fish — 2 lbs
   Clean, cut into 2" squares
2. Chili Powder — 3 tsp
3. Hot Chili Pepper — ½ tsp
4. Black Pepper — 1 tsp
5. Vinegar — 2 tsp
6. Oil — 1 cups to fry
   Salt to taste

PREPARATION:

Combine items 2-5. Season with salt. Marinate fish and leave it for an hour. Heat oil in a frying pan over high heat and deep fry the marinated fish on both sides till golden brown. Drain on paper towels.

FRIED FISH CURRY

1. Fish — 2 lbs
2. Onion — 2 cups thinly sliced
3. Ginger Root — 1" piece chopped
4. Garlic — 5 cloves chopped
5. Green Chili Pepper — 2 split the sides.
5. Tomatoes — 2 cut into four
6. Milk (Coconut Milk) — 1 ½ cups
7. Cream — ½ cup
8. Curry Leaves — 6
9. Oil — ½ cup
   Salt to taste

PREPARATION:

Fry the fish as in above recipe. Heat oil and deep fry onion to golden brown and set aside. Sauté ginger, garlic and green pepper for 2 minutes or till soft. Add curry leaves. Stir for a minute. Put in tomatoes and cook till soft. Add the fried fish. Stir for a while and pour in 1 ½ cup milk and ½ cup water. Cover and cook over medium heat for 10 minutes. Add ½ cup cream and fried onion. Bring to a boil and serve immediately. A very tasty dish that goes well with chappathi, corn or bread.

FISH BROWNIE

1. Fish — 1 lb
2. Onion — 1 cup cut into thin wedges
3. Shallots — 4
4. Ginger Root — ½" piece
5. Garlic — 3 cloves
6. Mustard Paste — 1 tsp
7. Green Pepper — 1
8. Green Chili Pepper — 2 deseeded
9. Vinegar — 1 Tbs
10. Bread Crumbs — 1 ½ cup
11. Oil to fry
    Mint Leaves
    Salt to taste

PREPARATION:

Grind ingredients 3-8 along with vinegar and salt. Marinate fish for 1 hour. Take marinated fish one by one, coat both sides in bread crumbs and deep fry on both sides till soft and brown over medium heat. Deep fry 1 cup onion in the remaining oil, drain and top it over the fried fish along with mint leaves.

SEA FOOD

BAKED FISH CRUNCH

1. Salmon Fillets	2 cups
2. Green Onion	2 Tbs
3. Chili Sauce	2 Tbs
4. Green Bell Pepper	1 chopped
5. Onion	½ cup chopped
6. Ginger Root	1 Tbs chopped
7. Carrots or Beets	½ cup grated
8. Butter	¼ cup
Salt to taste	

Pastry
1. All Purpose Flour   2 cups
2. Egg   1
3. Baking Powder   1 tsp
4. Black Pepper   ½ tsp
4. Cumin Seed powder   ¼ tsp
5. Margarine   ½ cup
Salt to taste   ½ tsp

Mix dry ingredients. Rub in margarine and mix well. Pour in the well beaten egg. Add ¼ cup warm water and knead well.

PREPARATION:

Melt butter. Sauté onion and ginger for a minute or till soft. Add green onion and pre-cooked salmon. Stir well and add all other ingredients. Stir fry for 2 minutes. Mix egg yolk and salt. Roll out a rectangle shaped pastry. Spread the salmon mixture on half side of the pastry and fold the opposite sides and seal the edges and brush the top with egg white. Bake the pastry at 350^0 F for 20 minutes or till golden brown.

SEA FOOD

SHRIMPS, LOBSTER, CRAB

SHRIMP/PRAWN CURRY

1. Prawns	2 lbs
2. Shallots or Onion	½ cup thinly chopped
3. Ginger Root	1" piece grated
4. Garlic	5 cloves crushed
5. Chili Powder	3 tsp
6. Hot Chili Powder	½ tsp
7. Turmeric	2 tsp
8. Tomato Paste	3 tsp
9. Tamarind	4 pieces
or Lemon Juice	3 Tbs
10. Fenugreek powder	½ tsp
11. Coconut	½ cup thinly cut in ¼" width
12. Coconut Milk	1 cup
13. Oil	4 Tbs
Salt to taste	

PREPARATION:

Heat oil in a thick bottomed pot and sauté onion till soft. Add ginger, garlic, and curry leaves and stir for 2 minutes over medium heat. Add tomato paste and stir-fry for 2 minutes over low heat. Add turmeric, chili powder, and fenugreek. Add 1 cup of water and salt. Add tamarind cut into small pieces. Bring to a boil and stir in the cleaned shrimps/prawns. Cover and cook for 5 minutes over medium heat. In 1 Tbs oil fry the

SEA FOOD

coconut pieces till light brown and add to the prawns curry while it is being cooked. When prawns become soft and sauce thickened add coconut milk. Heat well and serve.

Instead of tamarind lemon juice can be used. Adding Fenugreek leaves gives a special flavour

SHRIMP CHILI FRY

This easy-to-make dish is a favourite of all. It is flavourful and colourful.

1. Prawns — 2 lbs
2. Chili Powder — 2 tsp
3. Hot Chili Powder — ½ tsp
4. Vinegar — 1 tsp
5. Onion — 1 large thin slices
6. Ginger — 1" long grated
7. Black Pepper — ½ tsp
8. Butter or oil — 3 Tbs
   Salt to taste

PREPARATION:

Cook prawns with chili powders, salt, vinegar, and ½ cup water over medium heat. When all the liquid is absorbed, turn off heat. In a skillet, heat 3 Tbs butter or oil, add mustard then sauté onions till light brown. Add grated ginger and stir for a while. Add black pepper, cooked prawns, and stir-fry till all turn reddish brown.

SEA FOOD

YUMMY SHRIMP FRY

This is a favourite of all.

1. Shrimps   1 lbs (Large ones)
2. Rice flour   ¼ -½ cup
3. Hot Chili Powder   ¼ tsp
4. Parsley   2 Tbs (chopped fine)
5. Garlic paste   1 tsp
6. Ginger paste   ½ tsp
7. Black Pepper   ½ tsp
8. Olive oil   2 Tbs
9. Bread crumbs   1- 2 cups
10. Eggs   2
    Oil to fry
    Salt to taste

PREPARATION:

Peel and straighten the shrimps by making cuts on the bottom side. Mix olive oil, chopped parsley, garlic paste, ginger paste, Black pepper, Chili powder, and salt. Add the shrimps and leave it soaked in this mixture for an hour by keeping in the fridge. Take the shrimp one by one and cover in rice flour. Beat the eggs with a little water and soak the shrimps in egg mixture and cover in bread crumbs. Do soak the shrimp twice in egg mixture and coat in bread crumbs. Make oil

SEA FOOD

sizzling hot and deep fry.

To make it really crunchy after the first frying, fry them a second time. Use panko bread crumbs for better look.

Extra Recipe:

SEA FOOD

SHRIMP MASALA

1. Shrimps — 2 lbs
2. Onion — 2 one cut in to wedges
3. Ginger — 1" piece
4. Garlic — 5 cloves
6. Turmeric — ½ tsp
7. Fennel Seed Powder — ½ tsp
8. Cinnamon & Cloves — 1 tsp
9. Chili Powder — 2 tsp
10. Hot Chili — ½ tsp
11. Coriander Powder — 3 tsp
12. Coconut Milk — 2 cups
13. Tomato — 4
14. Oil — 3 Tbs
15. Black Mustard — 1 tsp
16. Curry Leaves — 6
    Salt to taste

PREPARATION:

Blend ingredients 3-11 along with one onion in a blender with ½ cup water. Place shrimps in a thick bottomed saucepan and pour in the puree. Add quartered tomatoes. Add salt and cook over medium heat for 3 minutes. Add coconut milk and simmer for 2 minutes. Heat oil in a frying pan and add mustard to pop. Add onion and curry leaves. Stir fry till onions turn golden brown. Add the shrimps stirring constantly for 2 minutes. Serve hot.

LOBSTER FRY

1. Lobster — 2 lbs
2. Onion — 2 cut thin lengthwise
3. Ginger Root — 1" piece chopped
4. Garlic — 5 cloves crushed
5. Chili Powder — 2 tsp
6. Hot Chili Powder — ½ tsp
7. Tomato Paste — 3 tsp
8. Chili Sauce — 1 tsp
9. Butter or Oil — 3 Tbs

Salt to taste.

PREPARATION:

Blend items 3-8 into a puree in a blender with ½ cup water. Pour in the puree into a saucepan and marinate the cleaned lobster. Season with salt and cook for 15-20 minutes or till lobster is done and all water absorbed. In a frying pan melt butter and sauté onion till light brown. Add lobster and stir-fry till they become reddish brown.

SEA FOOD

CURRIED LOBSTER

1. Lobster	2 lbs
2. Onion	1 chopped
3. Mustard Paste	1 tsp
4. Ginger Root	1" piece chopped
5. Garlic	4 cloves chopped
6. Chili Powder	1 tsp
7. Hot Chili Powder	½ tsp
8. Tomato Paste	4 tsp
9. Lemon Juice	3 Tbs
or	
Tamarind	4 small pieces
10. Fenugreek Powder	½ tsp
11. Curry Leaves	6
12. Coconut Milk	1 cup
13. Oil	3 Tbs
Salt to taste	

PREPARATION:

In a wok or skillet heat oil and sauté onion, ginger, garlic, and curry leaves for 5 minutes. Reduce heat to a minimum and add tomato paste. Stir-fry till paste is crisp for 3 minutes. Add mustard paste, chili powders, fenugreek powder, and turmeric and stir for 2 seconds. Add lemon juice or tamarind and 1 cup of water. Increase heat. Season with salt and when the mixture boils, add lobster. Cook for 6 minutes over medium heat. Add the milk when lobster is half-cooked (about 5 minutes). Serve hot with rice, corn or spaghetti.

SEA FOOD

BAKED LOBSTER

1. Lobster	2 lbs
2. Onion	1 sliced lengthwise
3. Garlic	5 minced or crushed
4. Mustard Paste	1 tsp
5. Chili Powder	1 ½ tsp
6. Black Pepper	1 tsp
7. Lemon Juice	1 tsp
8. Sugar	½ tsp
9. Coriander Powder	½ tsp
10. Butter	¼ cup
11. White Flour	3 Tbs
12. Water	½ cup
13. Yogurt	1 cup
Salt to taste	

PREPARATION:

Rub cleaned lobster with flour, chili powder, black pepper, salt, and mustard paste. Fry them in butter till light brown for 5-8 minutes. Keep them in a baking dish. In remaining butter, sauté onion and garlic for 3 minutes over medium heat. Add ½ tsp black pepper, coriander powder, and Lemon juice. Stir well. Remove from heat. Add yogurt, water and salt. Pour this mixture over the fried lobster and bake in the oven at 350° F for 30 minutes.

SEA FOOD

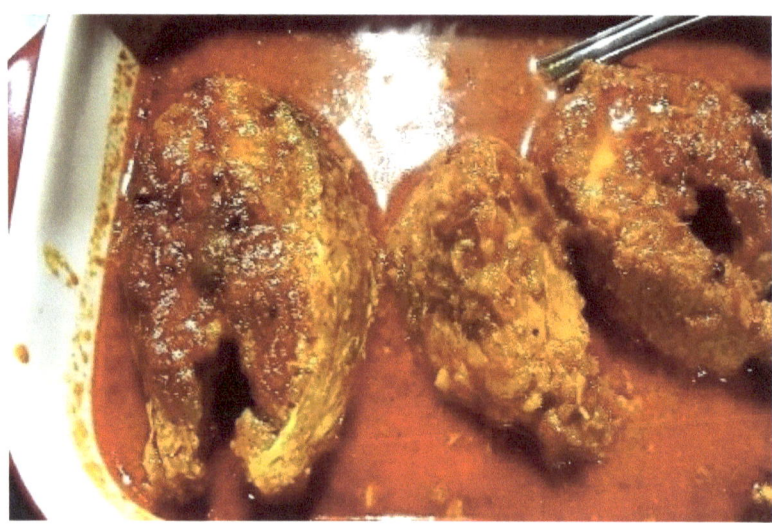

SEA FOOD

FAVOURITE CRAB DISH

1.	Crabs	4
2.	Onion	2
3.	Ginger Root	2" long
4.	Garlic	7 cloves
5.	Black Pepper	1 tsp
6.	Chili Powder	2 tsp
7.	Hot Chili	½ tsp
8.	Turmeric	½ tsp
9.	Coriander	3 tsp
10.	Tamarind	2 pieces
	or	
	Lemon Juice	4 tsp
11.	Oil	¼ cup to ½ cup
	Salt to taste	

PREPARATION:

Clean crabs well and cut to small pieces. Blend items 3-9 to a fine paste with some water (½ cup). Pour puree over the crab. Add ¾ cup water and tamarind. Season with salt. Cover and cook over medium heat till the crab is done and all liquid is evaporated. Stir occasionally. In a frying pan heat oil and sauté onion till soft and light brown. Add crabs and fry both sides. Serve hot.

For sauce, take ¾ cup freshly grated coconut, fry it over medium heat for 3 minutes and blend to a fine paste in ¾ cup water and add to the fried crabs. Bring to a boil.

SEA FOOD

CRAB COCONUT CURRY

1. Crabs   4
2. Onion   1 cut lengthwise and thin
3. Green Mango (raw) 1 (cut into small pieces)
   or
   Tamarind   3 piece
4. Chili Powder   2 tsp
5. Green Pepper   2 chopped
6. Green Chili Pepper 1 chopped
7. Turmeric   ½ tsp
8. Coriander   ½ tsp
9. Coconut (Shredded) 1 cup
   Salt to taste

PREPARATION:

Clean and cut crabs into small pieces. Combine green pepper, chili pepper, chili powder, coriander powder, and turmeric. Cut mango into small pieces and add. In a thick pot put these along with the crab. Add salt and 1 ½ cup water. Cook over medium heat for 15-20 minutes. Blend coconut to a fine paste with 1 cup water and add to the curry. Heat well and remove from heat before boiling.

VEGETABLES

VEGETABLES

BROCCOLI MUSHROOM DISH

1. Broccoli — 2 cups, cut in to cubes
2. Mushroom — 1 ½ cups, halved
3. Ginger Root — ¼" long chopped
4. Garlic — 3 cloves chopped
5. Onion — 1 cup sliced
6. Vegetable Oil — 2 Tbs
7. Black Pepper — ¼ tsp
   Salt to taste

PREPARATION:

Trim broccoli leaves and coarse stems. Wash and cut into short lengths. Wash and halve mushrooms. In ¼ cup water cook them covered for 4 minutes, along with ½ cup sliced onion and salt. In a frying pan heat oil and fry ½ cup onion till transparent. Add chopped ginger and garlic. Sauté for 2 minutes. Sprinkle black pepper and put the cooked broccoli and mushroom. Stir fry for 1 minute. Serve hot.

VEGETABLES

STRING BEANS AND POTATOES

1. Beans   2 cups, cut 2" long
2. Potatoes   2 cups, finger-sized
3. Chili Powder   1 tsp
4. Turmeric   ¼ tsp
5. Onion   1 cup, sliced thin
6. Green Chili Pepper   2 deseeded, halved
7. Lemon Juice   2 tsp
8. Vegetable Oil   3 Tbs
    Salt to taste

PREPARATION:

Trim ends and cut beans into 2 inch length. Peel and cut potatoes to finger size. Place them in a saucepan with ½ cup water. Add chili and ½ cup onion. Season with salt and chili powder. Cover and cook for 6-8 minutes. Let all water be absorbed. Heat oil in a frying pan and sauté the remaining sliced onion till transparent. Add turmeric and put in the cooked vegetables. Stir fry over medium heat for 3-4 minutes.

QUICK VEGETABLE CUTLET

A good treat for all occasions.

1. Vegetables   4 cups thinly chopped
2. Potato   3 cups mashed
3. Bread Crumbs   3 cups
4. Vinegar   1 Tbs
5. Eggs   2
6. Black Pepper   1 tsp
7. Ginger Root   1 Tbs grated
8. Onion   1 chopped
9. Oil for frying
   Salt to taste

PREPARATION:
Select vegetables of your choice (cabbage, carrot, radish, celery). Chop very thin or grate. Mix with cooked mashed potato. Add grated ginger, chopped onion, black pepper, vinegar, salt, and 1 cup bread crumbs. Separate egg yolk from egg white. Combine egg yolk with vegetables. Adjust seasoning. Make lemon sized, oval shaped patties, dip in egg white, soak with bread crumbs and deep fry both sides till golden brown.

VEGETABLES

LENTIL DISH

1. Lentils   1 cup
2. Water   2 cups
3. Black Mustard   ½ tsp
4. Onion   ½ cup chopped
5. Tomatoes   2 cut into cubes
6. Chili Powder   ½ tsp
7. Butter   2 Tbs
8. Turmeric   ½ tsp
9. Curry Leaves   7
   Salt to taste

PREPARATION:

Wash and soak lentils in hot water for 1 hour. Drain. Pour in 2 cups of water and salt, and cook till soft. Melt butter in a frying pan. Drop in mustard seeds. Add onion, curry leaves, and ginger. Sauté till onion becomes golden brown. Add cubed tomatoes. Reduce heat and stir in turmeric, ½ tsp chili powder. Add the cooked lentils. Adjust seasoning and serve hot.

VEGETABLES

MUNG BEANS CURRY

1. Mung Beans	1 cup
2. Coconut	1 cup grated
3. Green Chili Pepper	2 split the ends
4. Onion	¼ cup
5. Turmeric	½ tsp
6. Cumin Seed	¼ tsp
7. Garlic	3 cloves
8. Black Mustard	½ tsp
9. Butter	3 Tbs
10. Coconut	1 Tbs grated
11. Chili Powder or Red Chili	½ tsp / 1 broken to 4
12. Curry Leaves	10
Salt to taste	

PREPARATION:

Fry mung beans in a heavy bottomed pot till they become crisp and light brown in colour. Turn off heat. Wash and cook in 4 cups of water with salt for 30 to 35 minutes over medium heat. After 20 minutes put ¼ cup onion and split green chilies. When they become soft, mash well. Grind coconut, ¼ cup onion, turmeric, cumin and garlic in 1 cup warm water to a fine paste. Add it with mung beans and mix well. Stir and heat but do not boil. In a frying pan heat 3 Tbs butter and pop up mustard. Stir in chopped onion and grated coconut. Stir fry for 2 minutes or until onion and coconut turn light brown. Add curry leaves. When all turn golden brown, reduce heat and sprinkle ½ tsp chili powder and mix with mung beans curry. Serve with rice.

VEGETABLES

Do not mash green chilies, it may make curry very hot. Split skinned mung beans can also be used in the same way.

VEGETABLES

SAMBAR (VEGETABLE CURRY)

This is a good curry to eat with Idli and Dosa.

1. Lentils — 1 cup full
2. Potato — 2 cut into 8
   Carrots — 1 cup cut into 1" cubes
   Turnip — 1 cup cut into 1" cubes
   Cucumber & Beans — 1 cup each cut into cubes
3. Green Chili Pepper — 2 seeds removed halved
4. Coriander Powder — 3 Tbs
5. Hot Chili Powder — ½ tsp
6. Fenugreek Powder — ½ tsp
7. Asafetida — ¾ tsp
8. Onion — 1 large sliced
9. Black Mustard — ½ tsp
10. Curry Leaves — 2 sprigs
11. Tomatoes — 4 cut into four
12. Lemon Juice — 2 Tbs
13. Vegetable Oil — 2 Tbs
    Salt to taste

PREPARATION:

Soak lentils in water for an hour, wash and cook in 4 cups of water till soft. Mash it very well and set aside. Cut vegetables to 1" thickness and place in a heavy bottomed pot and cook in 2 cups of water and salt. When it boils add the green chilies, tomatoes and ¾ cup sliced onion. As all vegetables become tender remove from heat. Heat oil in a frying pan and pop up mustard. Add ¼ cup sliced onion and curry leaves. Stir fry till onion turns golden brown. Reduce heat.

VEGETABLES

Add coriander powder. Stir for a few seconds. Add turmeric, chili, and fenugreek. Combine. Mix cooked mashed lentils with vegetables. Add lemon juice and salt. Bring to a boil. Sprinkle Asafetida in, mix well, bring to a boil and serve.

VEGETABLES

BROWN CHICK PEAS

This is a very good preparation and I am sure that you would love it.

1. Chick Peas — 2 cups
2. Coriander Powder — 3 Tbs
3. Chili Powder — 1 tsp
4. Hot Chili Powder — ½ tsp
5. Garlic — 4 cloves
6. Fennel Seed Powder — ½ tsp
7. Cinnamon — ½ tsp
8. Turmeric — ½ tsp
9. Black Mustard — ½ tsp
10. Curry Leaves — 6
11. Tomato Paste — 1 tsp
    or
    Tomatoes — 2 medium chopped
12. Onion — 1 chopped
13. Coconut Milk — 2 cups
14. Vegetable Oil — 3 Tbs
    Salt to taste

PREPARATION:

Soak chick peas in water over night. Place in a saucepan and pour in 3 cups of water. Add salt. Cover and cook till soft. (Use a pressure cooker for quick cooking). In a skillet heat oil over fairly high heat and sauté mustard till they pop. Stir in onion and curry leaves. When onion turns light golden colour reduce heat and add tomatoes or tomato paste. Stir fry for 2 minutes. Add crushed garlic, coriander, chili powders

VEGETABLES

turmeric, and cinnamon and fennel seed powder. Stir fry for a few seconds. Add cooked chick peas and bring to a boil and simmer for 5 minutes. Pour the milk over and cook further for 2 minutes. Adjust seasoning and serve hot or cold with chappathi or parotta.

It is good to add ½ cup thinly sliced fresh coconut fried in 2 tsp butter along with the spices.

¼ tsp baking soda can be added to get it cooked quicker and softer. Good with any kind of breads, or spaghetti or chappathi. Cook large quantity and freeze.

VEGETABLES

GINGER CURRY

This is an effective, medicinal dish. Fresh ginger and tamarind used here gives a special flavour. A spoonful of this sauce will cure many of the stomach problems. Why not give a try!

1.	Ginger Root	1 cup peeled and grated
2.	Onion	½ cup chopped
3.	Garlic	4 cloves
4.	Coconut (fresh)	½ cup thinly sliced ¼ "long
5.	Chili Powder	2 Tbs (Paprika)
6.	Hot Chili Powder	1 tsp (optional)
7.	Green Chili Pepper	2 deseeded, chopped
8.	Tamarind Paste	1 Tbs
9.	Turmeric Powder	1 tsp
10.	Curry Leaves	10
11.	Black Mustard	1 tsp
12.	Tomato Paste	4 tsp
13.	Fenugreek Powder	½ tsp
14.	Vegetable Oil or Sesame Oil	½ cup
	Salt to taste	

PREPARATION:

Grate ginger or shred in a food processor. Heat oil and deep fry ginger. Drain and set aside. Place tamarind in 2 ½ cups of hot water and 2 tsp salt and leave for ½ an hour. In 2 Tbs oil fry sliced coconut till light brown. Set aside. Heat 1/4 cup oil over high heat and

VEGETABLES

add mustard to pop. Add chopped onion, green chili and curry leaves. Sauté till onion turn light brown. Add crushed garlic. Stir fry for a few seconds. Reduce heat and add tomato paste. Simmer for 1-2-minutes. Add turmeric powder, paprika, chili powder, and fenugreek. Sauté for 30 seconds stirring constantly. Mix tamarind well in the water and pour in. Increase heat. As the mixture boils add ginger and coconut. Add salt and adjust seasoning. Bring to a boil and simmer for 3 minutes. Stir occasionally. Cool and store.

VEGETABLES

RASAM OR MULAGUTHANNY

1. Tomato	4
2. Lentils (red)	¼ cup
3. Coriander Powder	1 tsp
4. Hot Chili Powder	½ tsp (optional)
5. Black Pepper	½ tsp
6. Turmeric	½ tsp
7. Fenugreek	½ tsp
8. Asafetida	¾ tsp
9. Garlic	5 cloves
10. Black Mustard	½ tsp
11. Onion	¼ cup
12. Curry Leaves	5
13. Lemon Juice	2 Tbs
14. Vegetable Oil	2 Tbs
Salt to taste	

PREPARATION:

Wash and pick over lentils. Place in a saucepan and add 4 cups of water. Cover and cook for 15 minutes or till soft. Add the whole tomatoes. Simmer for 10 minutes. When tomatoes and lentils become tender mash with a masher. Remove skins of the tomatoes. Put in crushed garlic and bring to a boil. Heat oil in a frying pan and add mustard to pop. Add chopped onion and curry leaves. Sauté for 2 minutes or till onion becomes golden brown. Reduce heat and add all spices (3-7) except Asafetida. Sauté and pour over the curry. Dribble lemon juice. Season with salt. Sprinkle Asafetida powder. Bring to a boil. Stir well and serve.

VEGETABLES

After adding Asafetida powder do not boil for a long time. You will lose the flavour.

VEGETABLES

CASHEW NUT CURRY

This is a very tasty and rich flavoured curry fit for all occasions.

1. Cashews   1 cup
2. Baking Soda   ¼ tsp
3. Chili Powder   ½ tsp
4. Coriander Powder   1 tsp
5. Cumin Seed Powder   ¼ tsp
6. Fenugreek   ¼ tsp
7. Green Chili Pepper   1 deseeded
8. Turmeric   ½ tsp
9. Tomato   1 chopped
10. Onion   ½ cup
11. Black Mustard   ½ tsp
12. Vegetable Oil   2 Tbs
13. Grated Coconut   1 cup
    Salt to taste

PREPARATION:

Cook cashews in 2 cups water and baking soda till soft. Dry fry grated coconut and ¼ cup sliced onion in a frying pan till light brown. Grind this coconut and onion to a fine dry paste in 1 cup water. Set aside. Heat 2 Tbs oil in a pot and pop up mustard. Add ¼ cup chopped onion and green pepper. Stir fry for 2 minutes. Reduce heat and add chili powder, coriander powder, turmeric, fenugreek powder, and cumin seed powder and sauté for a while. Season with salt. Add chopped tomato. Continue stirring. When tomato becomes soft add cooked cashews and stir gently. Add

VEGETABLES

pureed coconut and simmer for 2-3 minutes. Serve hot.

AVIAL

1. Vegetables:
   - Cucumber — ½ cup
   - Potato — ½ cup
   - Egg Plant — ½ cup
   - Beans — ½ cup
   - Turnips — ½ cup
   - Plantain (raw) — ½ cup
2. Onion — 1 cup
3. Green Chili Pepper — 2 ends split
4. Coconut — 1 cup grated
5. Cumin — ½ tsp
6. Garlic — 3 cloves
7. Yogurt — 1 cup
8. Coconut Oil — 1 Tbs
9. Turmeric — ¼ tsp
   Salt to taste

PREPARATION:

Cut vegetables into 2 inch length ½ inch thick. Place vegetables in a heavy bottomed pot. Pour 1 cup water. Add onion, green chilies, turmeric and salt. Cover and cook over medium heat for 7-to 10 minutes. Meanwhile grind coconut, cumin and garlic to a coarse paste in a blender with ½ cup water. Add ground coconut to the vegetables. Simmer for 2 minutes. Add yogurt and sprinkle salt over. Bring to a boil. Pour oil over, adjust seasoning and turn off heat.
Vegetables can be chosen according to availability and individual taste.

VEGETABLES

EGG PLANT FRY

1. Egg Plant   2
2. Chili Powder   2 tsp
3. Black Pepper   ½ tsp
4. Turmeric   ½ tsp
5. Ginger Root   ¼" long
6. Onion   ¼ cup
7. Oil   1 cup
   Salt to taste

Preparation:

Remove stalk and cut egg plant into 2 inch long thick slices. Soak in salted water for 2 minutes. Rinse and pat dry. Make a paste of ingredients 2-6 with salt and smear the dry pieces. Keep it for ½ an hour. Heat oil in a frying pan and fry on both sides till golden brown. Drain on paper towels and serve.

QUICK EGG PLANT FRY

This is a tasty and easy preparation.

1. Egg Plant   1
2. Egg   1
3. Black Pepper   ½ tsp
4. Lemon Juice   ½ tsp
5. Bread Crumbs   ½ cup
6. Vegetable Oil   1 cup
   Salt to taste

PREPARATION:

Cut egg plant in to thin rounds and place in salted water for 2 minutes. Drain and pat dry. Mix egg with pepper, Lemon juice, and salt. Take egg plant slices dip in egg mixture and coat with bread crumbs and fry on both sides till golden brown. Drain on paper towels and serve.

VEGETABLES

OKRA STIR-FRY

1. Okra   2 cups (cut thin & round)
2. Onion   1 cup cut in to strips
3. Green Chili Pepper 2 split deseeded
4. Chili Powder   ½ tsp
5. Vegetable Oil   4 Tbs
   Salt to taste

PREPARATION:

Trim off ends, wash and cut okra into thin rounds. Cut onion lengthwise to thin strips. In a non-stick frying pan heat oil and put in okra, onion, green pepper and salt. Stir fry for 2 minutes. Cover and simmer over medium heat for 2 minutes. Add chili powder. Stir fry till all become light brown and crisp.

Extra Recipe:

VEGETABLES

CABBAGE THORAN

1. Cabbage — 2 cups shredded
2. Onion — ½ cup chopped
3. Black Mustard — ½ tsp
4. Curry Leaves — 4
5. Green Chili Pepper — 1 cut lengthwise
6. Red Whole Chili — 1 broken to 3 (optional)
7. Garlic — 2 cloves finely chopped
8. Coconut Oil — 3 Tbs
9. Coconut — ½ cup grated
10. Turmeric Powder — ½ tsp
    Salt to taste

PREPARATION:

Cut cabbage to fine threads or shred in a food processor. Pour oil into a frying pan and add mustard to pop up. Add onion and curry leaves and stir fry till onion turns light brown. Reduce heat and add curry leaves, chili pepper, garlic, turmeric powder, and broken chili. Stir fry for 1 minute. Stir in grated coconut. Add shredded cabbage and salt. Increase heat and stir for 2-3 minutes. Remove from heat. Cabbage should not be overcooked. Serve hot.

Other vegetables like carrots, beet root, cauliflower, beans, spinach etc. can be cooked similarly.

VEGETABLES

SPICY POTATO FRY

A tasty side dish.

1. Potato (cut)   2 cups finger shaped
2. Onion   ½ cup thin slices
3. Coriander Powder   1 tsp
4. Fennel Seed Powder   ½ tsp
5. Cloves   ¼ tsp
6. Cinnamon   ¼ tsp
7. Black Pepper   ½ tsp
8. Chili Powder   ¼ tsp
9. Vegetable Oil   3 Tbs
   Salt to taste

PREPARATION:

Peel, wash, and cut potatoes. In ½ cup water mix ingredients 3-8 and add to potatoes. Season with salt and cook covered over medium heat till all water is absorbed and potatoes become tender. Remove from heat. Heat oil in a frying pan and sauté sliced onion till light brown. Stir in potatoes and stir fry for 4 minutes over medium heat till all turn brown and crisp. Serve hot.

CAULIFLOWER CURRY

1. Cauliflower   3 cups cut into 2" chunks
2. Potato   2 peel, cut into 6
3. Chili Powder   1 tsp
4. Coriander Powder   2 Tbs
5. Black Pepper   ½ tsp
6. Cumin Seed Powder   ¼ tsp
7. Cardamom Powder   ¼ tsp
8. Cloves   ¼ tsp
9. Cinnamon   ¼ tsp
10. Fennel Seed Powder ½ tsp
11. Turmeric   ½ tsp
12. Garlic   3 cloves crushed
13. Ginger Root   ½" long grated
14. Onion   ¾ cup sliced thinly
14. Lemon Juice   2 tsp
15. Coconut   1 cup grated
16. Curry Leaves   6
17. Butter   3 Tbs
18. Oil   ¼ cup
    Salt to taste.

PREPARATION:

Make a fine paste of ingredients 4 to 11 in ¼ cup water. Set aside. Smear cauliflower and potatoes with chili powder and salt. Heat ¼ cup oil in a frying pan. Add ½ cup onion, cauliflower, and potatoes. Stir fry all for 3 minutes. Pour lemon juice and salt. Leave aside. Heat butter and sauté ¼ cup onion till soft. Add ginger, garlic, curry leaves and the paste. Stir in the sautéed cauliflower and potatoes. Simmer in low heat for 3 to 5 minutes or till the vegetables are cooked. Make a

VEGETABLES

fine paste of coconut and mix with 1 cup 0f water and pour in. Adjust seasoning, bring to a boil. Serve hot with chapattis.

Extra Recipe:

VEGETABLES

SPICY MASHED POTATO

1.	Potato (medium)	4 peel, cut into 4
2.	Onion	½ cup chopped
3.	Green Chili Pepper	2 deseeded, chopped
4.	Coriander Powder	½ tsp
5.	Chili Powder	¼ tsp
6.	Turmeric	½ tsp
7.	Cloves Powder	½ tsp
8.	Ginger Root	1 tsp, chopped
9.	Vegetable Oil	3 Tbs
10.	Curry Leaves	6
11.	Black Mustard	½ tsp
	Salt to taste	

PREPARATION:

Cook potatoes in 1 cup water till soft. Turn off heat when all water is absorbed. Mash well. Heat oil in a frying pan and pop up mustard. Add onion, ginger, green chili, and curry leaves. Sauté for 2-3 minutes. Reduce heat and add all spices. Stir for a moment and stir in the mashed potato. Add salt. Combine well and serve.

VEGETABLES

VEGETABLE CUTLET (CLASSIC STYLE)

This is a tasty dish. Why not give a try!

1. Beans	½ cup grated
2. Carrot	1 cup grated
3. Turnip	½ cup grated
4. Cabbage	½ cup grated
5. Beets	¼ cup grated
6. Potato	2 cups, cooked, mashed
7. Onion	¼ cup chopped
8. Green Chili Pepper	1 chopped
9. Ginger Root	¼ "grated
10. Cloves Powder	¼ tsp
11. Eggs	2
12. Bread Crumbs	1 cup
13. Vegetable Oil	2 cups
14. Lemon Juice	1 Tbs
Salt to taste	

PREPARATION:

Heat oil in a wok and sauté onion, green pepper, and ginger for 3 minutes. Add grated beans and stir fry for 2 minutes. Add rest of vegetables and stir fry till all water is absorbed. Add cloves powder, Lemon juice, and salt. Remove from heat. Mix with the already cooked and mashed potato. Make square shaped cutlets. Dip in egg white soak with bread crumbs and deep fry on both sides till golden brown.

Enjoy this with tomato sauce, chili sauce or onion salad. Any vegetable can be used for making this dish.

VEGETABLES

SPINACH CUTLET

A fancy idea of making a real rich taste

1. Spinach   1 bunch
2. Potato   1 cup cooked, mashed
3. Onion   ¼ cup chopped
4. Ginger Root   ½ Tbs grated
5. Fennel Seed Powder   ¼ tsp
6. Black Pepper   ½ tsp
7. Butter   1 Tbs
8. Bread crumbs   1 ½ cups
9. Egg   1-2
10. Oil   2 cups
    Salt to taste

PREPARATION:

Trim off roots, wash and drain spinach. Cut them small and cook in an open pot with a little salt till all water is absorbed. Cook potatoes, and mash well. Sauté onion and ginger in 1 Tbs butter for 2 minutes. Add fennel and black pepper. Stir for a second and stir in mashed potato. Stir fry for 2 minutes and add dry cooked spinach and 3 Tbs bread crumbs. Separate white and yolk of the egg and mix the yolk with spinach. Adjust seasoning and make round balls and flatten them. Dip each one in egg white and soak with bread crumbs and deep fry on both sides till golden brown. Drain on paper towels and serve. You can make 20 cutlets.

Do not mix egg yolk with white. By using white alone you get more done and oil less bubbly. Instead of

VEGETABLES

potatoes cooked lentils can be used.

BITTER GOURD FRY

1. Bitter Gourd — 2 cups, cut thin & round
2. Onion — ½ cup, thinly sliced
3. Green Chili Pepper — 1 cut into 4
4. Lemon Juice — 2 tsp
5. Vegetable Oil — 1 ½ cups
6. Hot Chili Powder — ½ tsp (optional)
   Salt to taste

PREPARATION:

Cut bitter gourd round and thin. Remove the mature seeds from bitter gourd. Sprinkle lemon juice. Cut onion and green chili. Heat oil in a frying pan over high heat and add bitter gourd and green chili. Sprinkle with salt. Stir fry till all turn crisp and light brown. Drain on paper towels. In remaining oil fry onion slices till golden brown. Drain and spread over the fried bitter gourd.

Extra Recipe:

VEGETABLES

PUMPKIN DISH

1. Pumpkin (peeled) — 5 cups, cut into cubes
2. Green Chili Pepper — 2 ends split
3. Onion — 1 cup sliced thinly
4. Cumin Seed — ¼ tsp
5. Garlic — 3 cloves
6. Turmeric — ½ tsp
7. Coconut — 1 cup grated
8. Chili Powder — ½ tsp
9. Black Mustard — ½ tsp
10. Curry Leaves — 5
11. Urad Dal — ½ tsp
12. White Rice — ½ tsp
13. Butter — 3 Tbs

   Salt to taste

Preparation:

Peel and cut pumpkin into 2" long chunks. Cook in a heavy bottomed pot with ¼ cup water, ½ cup onion, green chili, and salt. When pumpkin become real soft mash it well keeping aside the green chili. Make a coarse paste of coconut, cumin, garlic, and turmeric in ¼ cup water. Mix it with the cooked mashed pumpkin. In a frying pan melt butter and pop up mustard. Add onion. As they turn golden brown add 1 Tbs grated coconut. Add urad dal and rice. Continue stirring. Add curry leaves. When all turn golden brown, reduce heat and add chili powder. Stir for a second and mix with cooked pumpkin. Stir fry for 1 minute. Season with salt and serve hot. It will be very thick with no sauce.

VEGETABLES

VEGETABLES

PLANTAIN FINGERS

A rare rich taste

1. Plantain — 2 peel, cut into finger shapes
2. Onion — 1 cup sliced thinly
3. Paprika — 1 tsp
4. Chili Powder — ½ tsp
5. Turmeric — ½ tsp
6. Vegetable Oil — 5 Tbs
   Salt to taste

PREPARATION:

Peel off the outer skin of plantain and cut into 2 inch long fingers. Place in salted water for 2 minutes. Rinse two to three times in fresh water. Drain. Add ½ cup water, salt, chili powders, turmeric, and ½ cup onion. Cover and cook over medium heat for 5-8 minutes or until plantain becomes soft. Turn off heat. In a frying pan pour in oil and sauté ½ cup sliced onion over high heat. Add banana fingers. Stir fry over medium heat for 3 minutes till all turn brown and crisp.

VEGETABLES

MUSHROOM DISH

1. Mushroom — 1 cup sliced
2. Coconut — 1 cup grated
3. Cumin Seed — ¼ tsp
4. Garlic — 2 small cloves
5. Green Chili Pepper — 1 chopped
6. Onion — 1 chopped
7. Turmeric — ¼ tsp
8. Black Pepper — ¼ tsp
9. Black Mustard — ½ tsp
10. Red Chili — 1 broken to 3
11. Coconut Oil — 2 Tbs
12. Curry Leaves — 6
    Salt to taste

PREPARATION:

Wash and cut mushroom to thin slices. Make a coarse paste of coconut, cumin, garlic, turmeric and ¼ cup onion. Add chopped green chili and black pepper. Mix mushrooms with coconut mixture. Add ¼ cup water and salt. Cook for 10 minutes. Let all water evaporate until dry. Remove from heat. In a frying pan heat oil and pop up mustard. Add onion and curry leaves and sauté till onion turns golden brown. Reduce heat. Add broken chili and mix with mushrooms. Stir and serve.

VEGETABLES

MUSHROOM CURRY

1. Mushroom	1 cup
2. Onion	1 large sliced
3. Green Chili Pepper	1 end split
4. Chili Powder	1 tsp
5. Hot Chili	¼ tsp
6. Cumin Seed	¼ tsp
7. Coriander	2 tsp
8. Turmeric	½ tsp
9. Fenugreek	¼ tsp
10. Tomato	2 chopped
11. Coconut	1 cup, grated
12. Vegetable Oil	4 Tbs
13. Curry Leaves	6
14. Black Mustard	½ tsp
Salt to taste	

PREPARATION:

Make a paste of ingredients 4-9. Sauté the paste in 2 Tbs oil over medium heat for 2 minutes. Add mushrooms and ½ cup sliced onion. Stir fry for 2 minutes. Add chili and tomatoes. Cook till tomatoes become soft. Cook for 2 minutes. Fry coconut for 2-3 minutes in a frying pan. Make a very fine paste of it and along with 1 cup water pour it into the mushroom. Heat well and set aside. Pop up mustard in 2 Tbs oil over a fairly high heat and add ½ cup chopped onion and curry leaves. Sauté till onion turns golden brown. Pour it into the curry.

PUMPKIN LEAVES THORAN

1. Pumpkin leaves — 3 (clean leaves with stem)
2. Coconut grated — 1 cup
3. Turmeric — ¼ tsp
4. Garlic — 2 cloves chopped
5. Onion — ½ cup chopped
6. Cumin Powder — ¼ tsp
7. Coconut Oil — 1 Tbsp
8. Mustard seeds — 1 tsp
9. Salt to taste

PREPARATION:

Pluck clean leaves from the pumpkin plant, wash drain, and put them together and slice them very thin. Heat coconut oil in a frying pan and add mustard seeds and cover to pop. Add chopped onion and garlic. Sauté till golden brown. Reduce heat. Add turmeric, cumin powder, and salt. Add the finely cut pumpkin leaves and grated coconut. Season with salt. Cook for 3 minutes till the leaves are softened and cooked.

It is very tasty to eat with Rice.

PICKLES, CHUTNEYS, CHIPS, SALADS

PICKLES

SWEET LEMON PICKLE

1.	Lemon	8
2.	Ginger Root	2 Tbs grated
3.	Garlic	½ cup cut into halves
4.	Green Chili Pepper	4 seeds removed
5.	Raisins	½ cup
6.	Sugar	1/4 cup
7.	Chili Powder	2 Tbs
8.	Hot Chili	1 tsp
9.	Mustard Paste	1 tsp
10.	Oil	1 cup
11.	Vinegar	1 cup
	Salt to taste	

PREPARATION:

Cut lemons into small pieces. Smear with salt and leave for one day. Heat oil and sauté ginger, garlic, and green pepper till they become soft. Add lemon and stir for 3 minutes. Add both chili powders and mustard paste. Make a paste of raisins in ½ cup water and add. Continue heating and when lemon becomes soft add sugar. Add vinegar. Let it boil and sauce be thickened. When cool store in bottles.

PICKLES, CHUTNEYS, CHIPS, SALADS

Extra Recipe:

LEMON PICKLE

1. Lemon — 6
2. Sesame Oil — 1 cup
3. Ginger Root — ½ cup chopped
4. Garlic — ½ cup cut into halves
5. Green Chili Pepper — 3 chopped
6. Turmeric — ½ tsp
7. Fenugreek Powder — ½ tsp
8. Asafetida — 1 Tbs
9. Chili Powder — 4 Tbs
10. Black Mustard — 2 Tbs
11. Hot Chili — 1 Tbs
12. Vinegar — 1 ½ cups
13. Curry Leaves — 10
    Salt to taste

PREPARATION:

Heat ¼ cup oil and sauté lemon, till they become soft. Cut one into four without separating it. Pour the remaining oil in a skillet and sauté ginger, garlic, green pepper, and curry leaves. When they become soft add crushed mustard and spices. Stir for a few seconds and add to the lemon. Season with salt. Boil vinegar, allow to cool. Arrange the lemon in a bottle and pour in the vinegar on top. Store when cool.

PICKLES, CHUTNEYS, CHIPS, SALADS

RAISINS LEMON PICKLE

1.	Lemon	4
2.	Raisins	½ cup
3.	Chili Powder	1 Tbs
4.	Hot Chili Powder	½ tsp
5.	Turmeric	½ tsp
6.	Fenugreek	½ tsp
7.	Asafetida	1 tsp
8.	Sugar	1 Tbs
9.	Mustard Paste	1 tsp
10.	Vinegar	½ cup
11.	Oil	½ cup
	Salt to taste	

PREPARATION:

Cut one lemon into 10 pieces. Heat oil in a wok and sauté lemon for 2 minutes. Add items 3-6. Stir fry for 5 minutes. Add raisins and mustard paste. Continue stirring. Add vinegar and sugar. Let it boil. As lemon becomes soft remove from heat. Sprinkle Asafetida and salt. Combine and store in bottles.

A good pickle for biriyani and fried rice.

PICKLES, CHUTNEYS, CHIPS, SALADS

MANGO PICKLE I

1. Green Mangoes — 4
2. Turmeric — ½ tsp
3. Mustard Paste — ½ tsp
4. Black Mustard — 1 tsp
5. Ginger Root — 1" piece
6. Garlic — ¼ cup
7. Raisins — ¼ cup
8. Vinegar — ½ cup
9. Sugar — 1 tsp
10. Oil — ¼ cup
    Salt to taste

PREPARATION:

Cut mangoes into small cubes and smear with salt and leave for two days. Stir it once or twice a day. After 2 days put in a strainer or colander to separate the sauce. Store the sauce. Pour oil in a skillet and pop up mustard over high heat. Make a paste of ingredients 2-7 in a blender and add to the skillet and stir fry for 3 minutes over medium heat. Add mango and continue stirring. Pour in the mango water, vinegar, and sugar. As it boils remove from heat. When cool, store.

MANGO PICKLE II

1. Green Mango — 6
2. Sesame Oil — ¾ cup
3. Ginger Root — 2" piece grated
4. Garlic — 1 cup cut lengthways
5. Mustard Paste — 1 tsp
6. Fenugreek — 1 tsp powder
7. Asafetida — 2 tsp
8. Paprika — 3 Tbs
9. Hot Chili — 2 tsp
10. Vinegar — 1 ½ cups
11. Curry Leaves — 12
    Salt to taste.

PREPARATION:

Cut mango into small cubes. Rub with ¼ cup oil and salt and leave for a day. Heat the remaining oil in a skillet or wok and sauté ginger, garlic, and curry leaves for 3 minutes. Reduce heat and add all spices items 5-9. Stir for a minute and remove from heat. Add previously boiled and cooled vinegar. When it is cool add mango and mix well. Adjust seasoning.

PICKLES, CHUTNEYS, CHIPS, SALADS

PRAWN PICKLE

1. Prawns — 1 lb
2. Black Mustard — 1 tsp
3. Ginger Root — 1" long
4. Garlic — ¼ cup
5. Green Pepper — ¼ cup
6. Turmeric — 1 tsp
7. Chili Powder — 4 Tbs (medium hot)
8. Fenugreek Powder — 1 tsp
9. Tomato Paste — 2 tsp
10. Vinegar — ½ cup
11. Boiled Water — ½ cup
12. Sesame Oil — 1 cup

Salt to taste

PREPARATION:

Marinate prawns with salt, 1 table spoon chili powder, turmeric, and 2 Tbs vinegar. After ½ an hour fry them in ½ cup oil till red brown. Add ½ cup oil to the pot. Make a paste of ginger, garlic, green pepper, and 1 tsp mustard. Sauté this paste in the oil for 3 minutes. Reduce heat and add tomato paste. Simmer for 3 minutes. Add the remaining spices. Stir for a minute. Drop in the fried prawns and stir well. Sprinkle boiled water. Bring the whole mixture to a boil. Remove from heat. Add previously boiled and cooled vinegar. Season with salt.

Use Paprika and Chili powder half and half to reduce the heat of the chili powder.

LOBSTER PICKLE

1. Lobster — 2 cups
2. Mustard Paste — 1 tsp
3. Ginger Root — 1 Tbs grated
4. Garlic — ¾ cup
5. Green Pepper — 2 cut thin and round
6. Black Pepper — 2 tsp
7. Chili Powder — 2 Tbs
8. Tomato Paste — 2 tsp
9. Turmeric — 1 tsp
10. Fenugreek — ½ tsp
11. Vinegar — ½ cup
12. Sesame Oil — 1 cup

Salt to taste

PREPARATION:

Make a paste of ginger and ½ cup garlic. Cut remaining garlic into halves. Smear lobster with tomato paste, salt, and black pepper and cook for 7 minutes. Let all water evaporate and be dry. Heat oil and sauté ginger and garlic paste for 3 minutes. Add lobster and stir fry for 2-3 minutes. Add halved garlic and mustard paste. Continue stirring. Reduce heat and add fenugreek powder, turmeric, and chili powder. Stir for a minute and remove from heat. Pour in boiled and cooled vinegar and ¼ cup boiled and cooled water. Mix and bottle when cool.

MEAT PICKLE

1. Beef — 1 lb cut into cubes
2. Ginger Root — 2 Tbs grated
3. Garlic — ½ cup
4. Green Pepper — 2 cut round and thin
5. Green Chili Pepper — 2 deseeded, chopped
6. All Spice — 1 tsp
7. Paprika — 3 tsp
8. Hot Chili — ½ tsp
9. Tomato Paste — 2 tsp
10. Black Mustard — 1 tsp
11. Oil — 1 cup
12. Fennel Seed Powder — ½ tsp
13. Black Pepper — 1 tsp
14. Vinegar — ½ cup

Salt to taste.

PREPARATION:

Cut meat into cubes. Season with salt and black pepper and deep fry till brown. Drain well. Make a paste of ¼ cup garlic, 1 Tbs ginger, and green chili pepper. In the remaining oil add mustard to pop up. Add remaining ¼ cup garlic cut into halves and green pepper and sauté for 2 minutes. Add tomato paste and ground ginger, garlic, and chili pepper. Stir for 2 minutes. Reduce heat and add chili powders, all spice and fennel seed powder. Turn in the meat. Continue stirring. Pour in vinegar and ½ cup boiled water. Allow the whole mixture to boil and simmer for 2 minutes. Adjust seasoning and store when cool.

BITTER GOURD PICKLE

1. Bitter Gourd — 2 cups (cut 1" long, thin)
2. Garlic — ¾ cup cut into halves
3. Ginger Root — ½ cup grated
4. Ground mustard — 1 tsp
5. Black Mustard — 1 tsp
6. Green Pepper — 2 cut 1" long
7. Green Chili Pepper — 3 cut round and thin
8. Fenugreek Powder — 1 tsp
9. Asafetida — ½ tsp
10. Vinegar — ½ cup
11. Oil — 1 cup
    Salt to taste

PREPARATION:

Fry bitter gourd in hot oil till they become soft and just cooked. Drain on paper towels. In the remaining oil pop up mustard and add items 2, 3, 6 and 7. Sauté for 3 minutes. Reduce heat and add fenugreek. Remove from heat. Add bitter gourd, mix with ground mustard and asafetida powder. Boil ½ cup water with 1 cup vinegar. Pour in when cool. Mix. Adjust seasoning.

CARROT PICKLE

1. Carrots — 3 cups
   Cut 1" long, finger-shaped
2. Garlic — ¾ cup cut into halves
3. Ginger — ¼ cup grated
4. Mango Powder — ¼ cup
5. Green Chili Pepper — 3 cut round and thin
6. Chili Powder — 1 Tbs
7. Black Mustard — 1 tsp
8. Turmeric Powder — ½ tsp
9. Asafetida Powder — 1 tsp
10. Sesame Oil — ¼ cup
11. Vinegar — ½ cup
    Salt to taste

PREPARATION:

Steam carrots in a steamer for 5 minutes. Grind ¼ cup ginger and ¼ cup garlic to a paste. Heat oil in a skillet and put mustard to pop. Add halved garlic, green chili, and the paste. Sauté for 3 minutes. Reduce heat to a minimum and add turmeric, mango powder, and chili powder. Put carrots in, stir for 1-2 minutes and remove from heat. Add Asafetida. Boil vinegar with ¼ cup water and pour in when cool. Mix well and store.

PICKLES, CHUTNEYS, CHIPS, SALADS

EGGPLANT PICKLE

1. Eggplant — 2 cups, finger shaped
2. Shallots — 2 medium chopped
3. Ginger Root — ¼" piece chopped
4. Garlic — ¼ cup crushed
5. Green Chili Pepper — 2 cut round and thin
6. Paprika — 1 Tbs
7. Hot Chili — ¼ tsp
8. Black Mustard — 1 tsp
9. Cumin Seed Powder — ½ tsp
10. Vinegar — ½ cup
11. Sugar — 1 Tbs
12. Sesame or Coconut Oil — ½ cup
    Salt to taste

PREPARATION:

Wash diced eggplant in salted water and drain. Heat oil and allow mustard to pop up. Add chopped shallot. When it turns light brown add ginger, garlic and green pepper. Sauté for 3 minutes. Reduce heat to a minimum and add all spices. Stir for a minute and add sugar. Stir in diced, drained eggplant. Let it simmer for 3 minutes. Add boiled vinegar and salt. Boil for a second. Cool and store.

GARLIC PICKLE

1. Garlic — 2 cups, peeled
2. Chili Powder — 3 tsp
3. Hot Chili — ½ tsp
4. Turmeric — ½ tsp
5. Black Mustard — ½ tsp (ground)
6. Fenugreek Powder — ½ tsp
7. Cumin Seed Powder — ¼ tsp
8. Asafetida — ¼ tsp
9. Onion — 1 Tbs chopped
10. Tomato Paste — 2 tsp
11. Vinegar — ½ cup
12. Vegetable Oil — ½ cup
   Salt to taste

PREPARATION:

In 2 table spoon oil sauté garlic for 2-3 minutes. Set aside. Make a paste of items 2-7. Heat oil and sauté onion for 2 minutes. Add the ground paste and tomato paste. Sauté for 3 minutes. Add salt and vinegar. Bring to a boil. Off heat and add garlic and salt. Sprinkle with Asafetida and combine all together.

PICKLES, CHUTNEYS, CHIPS, SALADS

FISH PICKLE

1. Fish   1 lb cut into small pieces
2. Ginger Root   1" piece
3. Garlic   6 cloves
4. Chili Powder   2 tsp
5. Black Pepper   1 tsp
6. Vinegar   2 Tbs
   Salt to taste

Make a fine paste of items 2-5 in vinegar. Add salt. Marinate fish in this paste for 2 hours. Bake at 450^0 F till light brown for 20-25 minutes.

1. Onion or Shallots   ¼ cup chopped
2. Ginger Root   1 Tbs grated
3. Garlic   ½ cup
4. Green Chili Pepper   3 chopped
5. Black Mustard   1 tsp ground
6. Chili Powder   3 tsp
7. Tomato Paste   2 tsp
8. Fenugreek Powder   ½ tsp
9. Vinegar   ½ cup
10. Turmeric   ½ tsp
11. Vegetable Oil   ½ cup
    Salt to taste

PICKLES, CHUTNEYS, CHIPS, SALADS

PREPARATION:

Crush ¼ cup garlic, grate ginger, and chop green pepper. Heat oil over high heat and sauté onion till light brown. Add crushed and whole garlic, ginger, and green pepper. Sauté for 3 minutes. Reduce heat and add turmeric, chili powder, and fenugreek. Turn off heat. Add fish and stir well. Stir in ground mustard and salt. Boil vinegar along with ¼ cup water and pour in when cool. Combine and store in bottle when cool.

PICKLES, CHUTNEYS, CHIPS, SALADS

CHUTNEYS

CARROT CHUTNEY

Nutritious, easy, tasty!

1. Carrots — 2 cups
2. Onion — ¼ cup
3. Green Chili Pepper — 2
4. Yogurt — 1 cup
5. Vegetable Oil — 2 Tbs
6. Black Mustard — ½ tsp
7. Onion — 2 Tbs chopped thinly
8. Ginger — ¼" chopped
9. Curry Leaves — 6
   Salt to taste

PREPARATION:

Dice carrots to small pieces and grind in the blender with yogurt, green chili, onion and ¼ cup water. Blend to a fine puree. Add salt. Heat oil in a frying pan over high heat and add mustard to pop up. Add thinly chopped onion, ginger, and curry leaves. When all turn light brown reduce heat and add carrot yogurt mixture. Warm and serve. Do not over heat.

> This is a very tasty and nutritious side dish. It goes very well with dosa and idli instead of coconut chutney.

TOMATO CHUTNEY

1. Tomatoes   2
2. Onion   ½ cup chopped
3. Ginger   2 tsp grated
4. Garlic   3 cloves
5. Green Chili Pepper 2
6. Chili Powder   ½ tsp
7. Oil   1 Tbs
   Salt to taste

PREPARATION

Bake tomatoes for 15-20 minutes or till soft and cooked. Smash well. Make a paste of ginger, garlic, ¼ cup onion, and chili pepper. Stir fry ¼ cup chopped onion in oil till light brown. Add the paste and stir fry for 1-2 minutes. Add chili powder and salt. Pour in the smashed tomatoes. Adjust seasoning and serve.

COCONUT CHUTNEY 1 (FOR DOSA & IDLY)

1. Coconut — 2 cups grated
2. Onion — ½ cup peeled and sliced
3. Green Chili Pepper — 2
4. Ginger Root — ½" piece peeled
5. Oil — 2 Tbs
6. Black Mustard — ½ tsp
7. Onion or shallot — ¼ cup, sliced
8. Curry Leaves — 5
9. Urad Dal — 1 tsp (optional)
10. Red Chili Pepper — 1
    Salt to taste

PREPARATION:

Grind items 1-4 in the blender with ½ cup water to a coarse paste. Add salt. Heat oil in a frying pan and add mustard to pop up. Stir in onion and curry leaves. Add urad dal. Sauté till onion turns light brown. Reduce heat to a minimum. Add one red chili broken to four pieces. Stir for a moment and pour coconut mixture into it. Combine well. Warm and serve.

COCONUT CHUTNEY 2 (SAMMENDY)

1. Coconut   2 cups
2. Onion   ½ cup
3. Ginger Root   ½" piece
4. Yogurt   1 Tbs
5. Red Chili Pepper   3 dry and roasted
6. Curry Leaves   5
   Salt to taste

PREPARATION:

Make a coarse paste of all ingredients by grinding in a blender. It is better to grind without water. Take it out and shape like a ball.

> Instead of red dry chili, ½ tsp chili powder and ½ tsp hot chili powder can be used. But it should be roasted over low heat for a few seconds before mixing with the coconut.

MANGO CHUTNEY

A good chutney for all occasions

1. Coconut   2 cups grated
2. Green Mango   ¼ cup sliced
3. Onion   ½ cup
4. Green Chili Pepper   3
5. Ginger Root   ½" piece
6. Coriander Leaves   2 Tbs
   Salt to taste

PREPARATION:

Cut mangoes into small pieces. Make a fine paste of all ingredients with ½ cup water in a blender. Garnish with coriander leaves.

MINT CHUTNEY

Take all ingredients as in mango chutney. Instead of mango pieces use ½ cup mint leaves.

PICKLES, CHUTNEYS, CHIPS, SALADS

BAKED FISH CHUTNEY

1. Fish Fillets — ¼ cup
2. Chili powder — ½ tsp
3. Hot Chili Powder — ½ tsp
4. Onion — ½ cup chopped
5. Ginger grated — ¼ cup
5. Lemon Juice — 1 tsp
6. Coconut Oil — 1 Tbs
   Salt to taste

PREPARATION:

Sprinkle fillets with chili powder on top and bake till soft and cooked. Blend or crush, chilies or chili powder, onion, ginger, salt, and lemon juice Add fish and mince. Combine with oil and serve.

Instead of chili powder red dry whole chilies or green chilies can be used. But bake or roast them before grinding. Green chilies can also be used. Those who prefer hot strong flavours can use a double amount of red or green chilies.

PICKLES, CHUTNEYS, CHIPS, SALADS

FISH MANGO CHUTNEY

Take ingredients as above and add ¼ cup fresh mango pieces before blending. Use 2 green chili pepper instead of red chilies.

BAKED CHUTNEY POWDER (SAMMENDY PODI)

1. Coconut — 2 cups grated
2. Onion — 1 chopped
3. Ginger Root — ½" piece chopped
4. Split Chick Peas — 1 tsp
5. Urad Dal — 1 tsp
6. Coriander Powder — ¼ tsp
7. Lemon peels — ¼ tsp
8. Black Pepper — ¼ tsp
9. Curry Leaves — 5
10. Chili Powder — 1 tsp
11. Hot Chili Powder — ½ tsp
12. Tamarind Paste — ½ tsp
    Salt to taste

PREPARATION:

In a baking tray place grated coconut, half of chopped onion, ginger, black pepper, lemon peels and curry leaves and bake at 350º F. Stir occasionally to see that it does not burn. When coconut turns light brown reduce temperature to 250º F. Add chili powders and coriander powder. When it turns little more brownish, remove from heat. In a frying pan fry chick peas and urad dal till crisp or light brown in colour. Grind them well. Add coconut mixture and continue grinding. When it seems to be oily put in the remaining onion and tamarind paste. Grind well all together. Add salt to taste.

This powder will remain for a long time. Double the quantity of hot chili powder to make it hot and spicy.

PICKLES, CHUTNEYS, CHIPS, SALADS

CHIPS

POPPADUMS

Poppadum or papad is a crunchy crispy wafer usually made out of urad dal, moong dal (black grams, lentils), potatoes or tapioca. Poppadums are bought ready to be used. It takes only a few seconds to be fried. It can be used either as a snack or as a side dish for any kind of meal.

1. Poppadum   4 break into four pieces
2. Vegetable Oil   1 cup for deep frying

PREPARATION:

Heat oil in a frying pan. When sizzling hot reduce heat and put poppadum one piece at a time holding with tongs deep into the oil. It will sizzle and expand within 2 seconds. Quickly turn over, cook for a second and drain on paper towels. Fry the rest similarly. Cooked poppadums will be crisp and golden.

Poppadums can be made ahead of time and reheated in a hot oven uncovered for 1-2 minutes at 350^0 F. They can be stored in air tight containers to keep them crunchy.

PICKLES, CHUTNEYS, CHIPS, SALADS

TAPIOCA WAFER

1. Tapioca Wafer   4
2. Vegetable oil   1 cup

PREPARATION:

Heat oil in a frying pan. When oil is sizzling hot insert tapioca wafer into hot oil holding with tongs. It will double in size. Quickly turn over and cook for a second. Take out and drain on paper towels.

BANANA CHIPS

1. Raw green Plantain   2
2. Vegetable oil   1-2 cups
3. Salt to taste

Peel the skin of banana and cut into thin, round slices. Heat oil and fry them till golden brown. Sprinkle salt on the hot chips. Enjoy!

Extra Recipe:

PICKLES, CHUTNEYS, CHIPS, SALADS

SALADS

TOMATO ONION SALAD

1. Tomatoes — 3
2. Onion — ½ cup sliced
3. Green chili — 1 deseeded, chopped
4. Yogurt — 1 cup
   Salt to taste

PREPARATION:

Wash and cut tomatoes round and thin. Mix with chopped green chilies. Slice onion thin and round. Place sliced onion in salted water for 2 minutes. Squeeze off water and add to tomatoes. Pour in yogurt and salt. Combine and serve.

CABBAGE COCONUT SALAD

1. Cabbage   1 cup, grated
2. Onion   ¼ cup, chopped
3. Coconut   ½ cup, grated
4. Lemon Juice   1 tsp
   Salt to taste

PREPARATION:

Chop onion and keep in salted water for 2 minutes. Squeeze off water. Add to grated cabbage. Add fresh grated coconut. Pour in lemon juice and salt. Combine and serve.

CUCUMBER SALAD

1. Cucumber — 1 medium
2. Peanuts — 3 Tbs roasted, crushed
3. Coconut — 3 Tbs grated
4. Lemon Juice — 1 ½ Tbs
5. Green Chili — 1 chopped
6. Asafetida — a pinch
7. Black Mustard — ½ Tsp
8. Chili Powder — ¼ tsp
9. Sugar — 1 tsp
10. Vegetable Oil — 2 tsp
    Salt to taste

PREPARATION:

Peel and cube the cucumbers. Combine with roasted, shelled and crushed peanuts. Add coconut, lemon juice, sugar, green chili and salt. Heat oil in a pan and pop up mustard. Reduce heat and add Asafetida. Add chili powder. Stir and pour it hot over the relish. Combine and serve.

PICKLES, CHUTNEYS, CHIPS, SALADS

PRAWNS SALAD

1. Prawns   ½ lb
2. Lemon Juice   3 Tbs
3. Coconut Milk   ½ cup
4. Garlic   2 crushed
5. Green Onion   2 Tbs chopped
6. Green Chili Pepper   1 deseeded, chopped
7. Green Pepper   ½ cut in rounds
8. Tomato   1 cut thin and round
9. Parsley   1 Tbs
   Salt to taste

PREPARATION:

Place the cleaned and sliced prawns in a salad bowl. Add lemon juice. Add parsley thinly chopped. Season with salt. Add crushed garlic green chili pepper and onion. Stir well and pour in the thick coconut milk. Refrigerate for 12 hours. Just before serving garnish the top with green pepper and tomato rings.

SNACKS

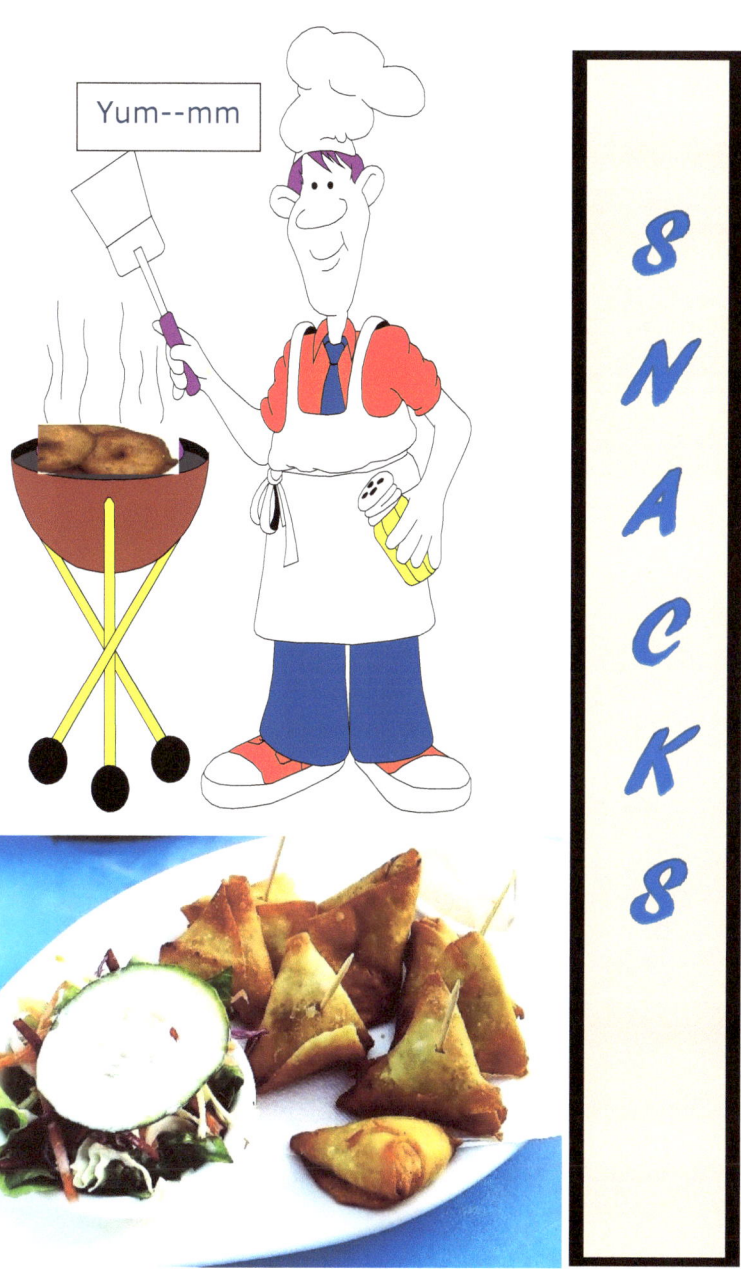

SNACKS

BAKED SAMOSA

A crowd pleaser!

1. White Flour — 2 cups
2. Butter — ½ cup
3. Milk — ½ cup
4. Egg — 1
5. Lemon Juice — ½ tsp
6. Baking Powder — 1 tsp

FILLING
1. Potato — ¾ cup mashed
2. Peas (frozen) — ½ cup
3. Carrots — ½ cup
4. Onion — ½ cup sliced thin
5. Green Chili Pepper — 1 chopped
6. Ginger — ½" chopped
7. Coriander Powder — ½ - 1 tsp
8. Fennel Seed Powder — 1 tsp
9. Turmeric — ½ tsp
10. Vegetable Oil — 3 Tbs
    Salt to taste

PREPARATION:

Sift flour with baking powder and salt. Make a firm dough with butter and milk. Cover it with a plastic wrap and let stand for ½ to 1 hour. Dice carrots into ½" cubes. Pour oil in a frying pan and sauté sliced

SNACKS

onion, grated ginger, and green chili. When they become soft add turmeric, fennel, and coriander powder. Stir for a while and add diced carrots and peas. Add a little salt. Reduce heat and cook covered for 2 minutes. Uncover and add the mashed potatoes. Stir fry for a minute and set aside. Break dough into small egg size balls. Roll them out to thin circles. Cut each in the middle. Fill each semicircle with the filling and fold one end to the other to form a triangular, cone shaped samosa. Seal edges with white of the egg or little milk. Brush egg white on top of each samosa and bake in a pre-heated oven at 350^0 F till golden for 25-30 minutes.

Samosas freeze very well. Brush egg white only at the time of baking. Any vegetable can be taken as the filling. Ground beef can be used as the filling in place of vegetables.

SNACKS

UZHUNNU VADA (URAD DAL VADA)

Savory & nutritious.

1. Urad Dal — 2 cups
2. Onion — 1 cup chopped
3. Ginger Root — 1 Tbs grated
4. Green Chili — Pepper finely chopped
5. Chili Powder — ½ tsp
6. Curry Leaves — 5 cut into half
7. Coriander Leaves — 2 Tbs, chopped
8. Baking Soda — ¼ tsp
8. Oil for frying — 2-3 cups
   Salt to taste

PREPARATION:

Soak urad dal in warm water for 4 hours. Drain well. Blend to a fine paste with two table spoons of water. Add baking soda to the thick batter. Add ingredients 2-7. Season with salt. Combine. Soak hand in medium hot water place one egg size ball in hand, flatten slightly. Make a hole in the centre with your finger. It should look like a donut. Gently put the donut shaped ball into the sizzling hot soil and deep fry. Reduce heat slightly. When one side is cooked turn over. When both sides turn golden, take out with a slotted spoon. Repeat the process. Drain on paper towels. Serve hot with coconut chutney and sambar (vegetable curry)

To make onion vada, add one more cup of chopped onions to the batter.

SNACKS

SNACKS

PARIPPU VADA

Savory & nutritious.

1. Split Chickpeas
    (Chana Dal)   2 cups
2. Onion   1 cup chopped
3. Ginger Root   1 Tbs grated
4. Green Chili Pepper   1 chopped
5. Chili Powder   ½ tsp
6. Curry Leaves   6
7. Coriander Leaves   2 Tbs, chopped
8. Asafetida Powder   ½ tsp
9. Baking Soda   1/8 tsp

Oil for frying   2-3 cups
   Salt to taste

PREPARATION:

Soak chana dal in warm water for 4 hours. Drain. Blend to a coarse paste without any water. Add ingredients 2-9. Season with salt. Combine. Make egg size balls, flatten by pressing between palms. Deep fry in sizzling hot oil. Reduce heat to medium. When one side is cooked turn over. When both sides turn golden, take out with a slotted spoon. Repeat the process. Drain and serve.

SNACKS

CREAM OF WHEAT DELIGHT

Real yummy treat!

1. Cream of Wheat   2 cups
2. Butter   ¼ cup
3. Fresh Coconut   1 ½ cup grated
4. Sugar   1 ½ cup
5. Rice Flour   ½ cup
6. White Flour   ½ cup
7. Milk   ½-¾ cup
8. Cumin Seed   1 tsp (optional)
9. Oil for frying
   Salt to taste

PREPARATION:

Put cream of wheat into a baking dish. Dot with butter. Bake at 350^0 F till it changes color and crispy. Stir in between. Add grated coconut. Mix and bake for further 3-5 minutes. Take out and put into a heavy bottomed pot. Heat. Add sugar. Continue stirring. When sugar starts melting pour in ½ cup of milk and turn off heat. Combine thoroughly and make balls when mixture is cool. Make a batter with rice flour, white flour and ½ cup of water. Season with cumin and salt. Soak each ball in the batter and deep fry both sides. Drain on paper towels.

PLANTAIN DELIGHT (ETHEKA APPAM)

Easy, quick and delicious! Select ripe and soft plantain.

1. Plantain   2 peeled
2. White Flour   ¾ cup
3. Rice Flour   ½ cup
4. Honey (optional)   2 Tbs
5. Water   ½ cup
6. Baking Soda   1 pinch
   Vegetable Oil to fry
   Salt to taste

PREPARATION:

Remove skin from ripe soft plantain. Cut one plantain horizontally into 3. Cut vertically each piece to 3 thin slices. Make a batter with ingredients 2-6. Add salt to taste. Heat oil in a frying pan.

SNACKS

Dip each plantain in the batter and deep fry both sides till golden yellow. Drain on paper towels.

UNNIAPPAM

1. White Flour — 1 cups
2. Cream of Wheat — ½ cup
3. Rice Flour — ½ cup
4. Pancake Flour — ½ cup
5. Brown sugar — 4 Tbs (Jaggery)
6. Coconut Fresh — ½ cup sliced thin, small
7. Cardamom — ½ tsp
8. Ginger Powder — ¼ tsp (dry)
9. Baking Soda — ¼ tsp
   Vegetable Oil for frying
   Salt to taste

PREPARATION:

Dissolve jaggery (Indian brown sugar) in two cups of water. Combine all the flours. Add cardamom, ginger powder, baking powder and salt. Fry thinly sliced coconut in 2 tablespoon oil to golden brown. Add to the batter. Season with salt. Heat oil in a frying pan or wok and when oil is sizzling hot, pour 1 table spoon batter into the oil. It will double in size and rise up. Turn over. When both sides turn brown take out with a slotted spoon and drain. Serve along with tea.

BANANA UNNIAPPAM

1. Ripe Bananas   2-3
2. Rice Flour   ½ cup
3. White Flour   1 cup
4. Cream of Wheat   ½ cup
5. Brown Sugar or
   Jaggery   ½ cup
6. Cardamom Powder   ½ tsp
7. Water   1 cup
8. Baking Soda   ¼ tsp
   Oil for frying
   Salt to taste

PREPARATION:

Mash bananas well. In 1 cup water make a batter with ingredients 2-8. Mix with mashed bananas and salt. Set aside for 1 hour. Heat oil to sizzling hot and pour 1 tablespoon batter and deep fry both sides. Drain and serve.

SNACKS

PLANTAIN FRITTERS

1. Plantain   2
2. Honey   2 Tbs
3. Butter   ½ cup

PREPARATION:

Peel ripe plantain. Cut in the middle. Make thin slices. Melt butter in a frying pan and fry each slice golden brown at medium heat. Drain and brush honey over it.

SNACKS

VEGETABLE PATTIES

1.	Beans	½ cup
2.	Carrots	½ cup
3.	Peas	¼ cup
4.	Celery	¼ cup
5.	Onion	½ cup
6.	Green Chili	1 deseeded, chopped
7.	Bread	1 loaf
8.	White Flour	1 Tbs
9.	Lemon Juice	2 tsp
10.	Black Pepper	½ cup
	Oil for frying	
	Salt to taste	

PREPARATION:

Dice all vegetables to ½" cubes. Sauté chopped onion and green chili in 2 Tbs oil till onion turn light brown. Add all vegetables and stir fry till soft. Add lemon juice, black pepper and salt. Let all water be evaporated. Trim off sides from bread slices. Soak one by one in water for a moment, take out and press very well keeping in between the palms to drain off all water. Stuff 1 Tbs filling in each piece and cover with another. Mix white flour in a little water. Seal the edges of the stuffed bread slices with the batter. Shallow fry in medium heat till golden. Drain on paper towels and serve.

SNACKS

PEANUT CRISPS

A simple snack for kids

1. Peanuts   2 cups
2. White Sugar   ¾ cup
3. Water   1/2 cup

PREPARATION:

Put peanuts, sugar, and water into a pot. Stir fry till all water is evaporated and sugar coats on the peanut. Reduce heat and continue stirring. The sugar will turn light brown forming a coating over the peanuts without sticking to each other. Remove from heat and spread on trays. Stir for some time. When cool, store in sealed jars.

Extra Recipe:

SNACKS

SESAME BALLS

1. Sesame Seeds   1 cup
2. Butter   2 Tbs
3. Lemon Juice   ½ tsp
4. Coconut   ½ cup grated
5. Jagggery   ¾ cup

PREPARATION:

Fry sesame seeds in butter till they become crispy. Heat Indian molasses or jaggery, coconut and 3Tbs water over medium heat. When syrup reaches a thread like consistency, turn off heat and pour lemon juice. Combine with sesame seeds. Stir well. Make balls when mixture is cool and manageable.

Extra Recipe:

SNACKS

GULAB JAMAN

1. Powdered Milk   1 cup
2. Baking Powder   ½ tsp
3. Egg   1 medium
4. White Flour   1 Tbs
5. Butter   1 Tbs
6. Sugar   1 cup
7. Cardamom   2 pods

PREPARATION:

Knead flour, milk powder, baking powder, butter, and egg. Sprinkle a little water to make a soft firm dough. Knead well. Make small balls and deep fry on low heat. Boil sugar, cardamom pods and 2 cups water together. When both sides of the balls are golden brown take them out and put them straight into the sugar syrup. When all balls are done bring syrup to a boil and turn off heat.

SNACKS

BAKED BANANA PUFFS

A tasty pastry.

1. White Flour — 2 cups
2. Baking Powder — 1 tsp
3. Melted Butter — ¼ cup
4. Eggs — 2
5. Butter Milk — 1/4 cup
6. Coconut — 1 cup grated
7. Banana — 3 mashed
8. Sugar — 2 Tbs
9. Cardamom Powder — ½ tsp
10. Cream of Wheat — 1 Tbs
11. Corn Starch — 1 Tbs
    Salt to taste

PREPARATION:

Sift together baking powder, salt and white flour. Add melted butter and one egg. Pour in buttermilk little by little and form a soft firm dough. Roll dough into a thin layer. Cut into small rounds with a biscuit cutter. Mash bananas and mix with coconut, sugar, Cream of wheat, corn starch, and cardamom powder. Stuff each round with a teaspoon full of banana mixture. Fold rounds and seal the middle edges with beaten egg. Brush top and sides with egg mixture and bake in a pre-heated oven till golden at 375^0 F for 10-15 minutes.

SNACKS

PEA FLOUR FUDGE

1. Chick Pea Flour   2 cups
2. Butter   1 cup
3. Sugar   1 ½ cups
4. Water   1 ¼ cups
5. Nuts   1 cup
   Chopped (cashews/almonds)
6. Cardamom Powder   ½ tsp
7. Nutmeg Powder   ½ tsp
   Salt to taste

PREPARATION:

Measure flour. Melt butter in a heavy bottomed pan and stir in the flour. Stir fry till the flour turns light brown (5-7 minutes). Remove from heat. Meanwhile in another pan make a sugar syrup with water and sugar. Bring to a boil. Continue boiling till syrup becomes thick and forms a thread like consistency (if a drop is pressed between the thumb and finger a strand would form). Add salt to sugar syrup. Add fried flour slowly to the syrup. Reduce heat and stir continuously for 3 minutes until mixture comes away from the pan. Add nuts and stir for few seconds. Turn off heat. Sprinkle the spices. Stir well. Empty contents into a greased dish or tray. Smoothen the surface with a wet spoon. Cut into any desirable shape.

It is better to roast nuts in 1 table spoon butter before adding.

RICE FUDGE

1. Rice Flour — 2 cups
2. Coconut Milk — 2 cups
3. Butter — 3 Tbs
4. Egg — 1
5. Jaggery — 1 ½ cups (Brown Sugar)
6. Cream — ½ cup
7. Cumin Seed Powder — ½ tsp
8. Cardamom Powder — ½ tsp
9. Cashews (broken) — ½ cup chopped
   Salt — ¼ tsp

PREPARATION:

Make a batter with rice flour and milk. Add Brown sugar. Cook on medium heat. Whisk egg and pour in. Stir constantly. Be careful that it does not stick to bottom. When it boils add butter. Continue stirring till rice is cooked and thickened. Boil cream in another pot and add in. Stir for further 2 minutes. Turn off heat. Add nuts and spices. Mix very well. Spread it on a greased baking dish. Bake at 350^0 F in the centre of oven for 25 minutes or till top is light brown. Cool and cut.

SNACKS

CREAM OF WHEAT LADU

1. Cream of Wheat   2 cups
2. Sugar   1 cup
3. Butter   6 Tbs
4. Blanched Almonds ¼ cup chopped
5. Cashews   ¼ cup chopped
6. Nutmeg Powder   1 tsp
7. Milk   ¼ - ½ cup

PREPARATION:

Fry cream of wheat in butter for 5 minutes or till they are crisp. Add sugar and nuts. Stir fry further for 3 minutes. Add nutmeg powder. Pour in milk, stir and turn off heat. When it is manageable make lime-size balls.

Extra Recipe:

SNACKS

CREAM OF WHEAT COCONUT PASTRY

1. Cream of Wheat   ½ cup
2. Coconut   ½ cup
3. Butter   3 Tbs
4. Sugar   ½ cup
5. Cardamom Powder   ½ tsp
6. White Flour   2 cups
7. Eggs   2
8. Oil or Butter   ½ cup
9. Butter Milk   ¼ -1/2 cup
10. Baking Powder   1 tsp
    Salt to taste

PREPARATION:

Fry or bake cream of wheat along with butter till light brown or crisp. Add grated coconut and stir fry for 2 minutes. Add sugar. Continue stirring till sugar starts melting (1-2 minutes). Set aside. Turn off heat. Make a firm dough with flour, baking powder, one egg, one egg yolk, butter, butter milk and salt. Keep one egg white separate for brushing over pastries. Make small balls. Roll it thin and round. Brush ½ tsp oil on the top. Fold in half. Spoon in the cream of wheat mixture in the middle. Fold opposite sides and seal edges with egg white. Brush the top with egg white. Make all in the same manner and bake in a pre-heated oven at 375^0 F for 15-20 minutes.

SNACKS

MEAT PUFFS

A crunchy rich taste.

1. Ground Beef — 2 cups
2. Onion — 1 chopped, medium
3. Ginger Root — 1" piece grated
4. Worcester Sauce — 1 Tbs
5. Black Pepper — ½ tsp
6. Cloves Powder — ¼ tsp
7. Potato — 1 cup mashed
8. Butter — ¼ cup
9. Frozen Puff Pastry — 250 gms

Salt to taste

PREPARATION:

Cook meat with salt and vinegar till soft and mince. Heat 2 table spoon butter or margarine in a frying pan and stir fry onion and ginger. When it becomes soft, add cloves and black pepper. Stir in meat and stir fry for 2 minutes. Pour in Worcester sauce and salt. Turn off heat and add mashed potato. Combine well. Divide pastry sheets into squares (9 or 10). Fill each square with meat mixture. Fold the sides. Seal edges with egg white. Brush egg white on top and bake at 375^0 F for 20-25 minutes.

ONION PAKKODA

1. Chick Pea Flour   1 cup
2. Rice Flour   ¼ cup
3. Onion   1 cup sliced thin
4. Plain Yogurt   ¼ cup
5. Ginger Root   ¼" long chopped
6. Cayenne Pepper   ½ tsp
7. Turmeric   ¼ tsp
8. Salt   ¾ tsp
9. Water   1 cup
10. Cumin Powder   ½ tsp
    Oil for deep frying

PREPARATION:

Make a batter with rice flour, chick pea flour, yogurt, and water. Add ingredients 5-10. Stir in the sliced onion. Heat oil in a deep fat fryer. Drop gently each onion slice coated with the batter into the sizzling oil and fry both sides for 1-2 minutes till golden brown. Drain and serve.

Cauliflower, eggplant, and spinach can be substituted in place of onion.

SNACKS

POTATO BHAJI

1. Chick Pea Flour   1 cup
2. Chilly Powder   ½ tsp
3. Asafetida Powder   ¼ tsp
5. Lemon Juice   1 tsp
6. Potatoes   3 sliced round and thin
7. Turmeric   ¼ tsp
8. Salt   ½ tsp
   Oil for deep frying

PREPARATION:

Combine ingredients 1-5. Add salt and turmeric. Pour in 1 cup of water and make a smooth batter. Heat oil in a deep fat fryer. Dip each potato piece in the batter and deep fry on both sides till golden.

Raw plantains, cauliflower, egg plant, onion etc. can also be used.

SNACKS

BONDA

1. Potatoes   2 cups mashed
2. Green Chili Pepper 1 deseeded, chopped
3. Onion   1 cup chopped
4. Black Mustard   ½ tsp
5. Ginger Root   ¼" grated
6. Fennel Seed Powder ½ tsp
7. Chili Powder   ¼ tsp
8. Turmeric   ¼ tsp
   Salt to taste

PREPARATION:

Heat 3 table spoon oil in a frying pan and add mustard to pop. Add chopped onion, ginger, and green chili. Sauté for 2 minutes or till all turn light brown. Add fennel seed powder, turmeric, and chilly powder. Stir for a moment and put in the mashed potato. Stir well and turn off heat. Make small balls when cool and dip in bhaji batter (as in Potato Bhaji) and deep fry on both sides till golden. Drain and serve.

SNACKS

CRISPY COOKIES (MURUKKU)

1. Chick Pea Flour   ½ cup
2. Rice Flour   ½ cup
3. Black Gram Flour
   (Urad Dal Flour)   ½ cup
4. Asafetida Powder   ¼ tsp
5. Cumin Seed Powder   ¼ tsp
6. Cayenne Pepper   ¼ tsp
7. Turmeric   ¼ tsp
8. Vegetable Oil   1 Tbs
   Salt to taste
   Oil for frying

PREPARATION:

Mix ingredients 1-8. Pour in ½ cup of warm water and make a smooth dough. Put dough into the murukku mould with medium hole plate and press into the hot oil and make round shapes. Deep fry till crispy. Drain and store in air tight containers.

Moulds are available in oriental stores.

SNACKS

WHITE HALVA

Halva making is a real art. It is rich and tasty!

1. Cake Flour   1 cup
2. Milk   ½ cups
3. Honey   1 ½ cups
4. Ghee   ¾ cup
5. Cardamom   ¼ tsp
6. Nutmeg Powder   ½ tsp
7. Cashews (broken)   ¼ cup

PREPARATION

Make a batter with cake flour and milk in a non-sticking pan. Blend to a smooth texture. Pour through a colander. Add honey and bring to a boil stirring constantly. Reduce heat and add 1 table spoon ghee at a time. Do not allow the mixture to stick to the bottom. When the mixture becomes very thick, add chopped nuts. Take a spoonful and when cool, check if a small ball can be made without being sticking to the hand. Sprinkle the spices and mix well. Take out and spread on a greased tray. Smoothen the surface. Cut when cool. It takes only 40-45 minutes to make this.

CARROT HALVA

1. Carrots — 2 cups grated
2. Sugar — 2 ½ cups
3. Butter — 1 cup
4. Milk — 3 cups
5. Cake Flour — 1 cup
6. Cashews (broken) — ½ cup
7. Cardamom Powder — 1 tsp

PREPARATION:

Add 1 cup of milk to the grated carrot. Cover and cook in a non-sticking pan. Stir at times. After 5 minutes add sugar and start continuous stirring. Make a batter with flour and 2 cups of milk. Pour it through a colander to see that it is a smooth batter. Pour it gently on the boiling carrots. Add ¼ of butter to the mixture and continue stirring. As it is thickened add the remaining butter little by little. Add cardamom powder and nuts. Check the doneness and if it is not sticking between your fingers, remove from heat and spread in a greased tray. Level the surface.

SNACKS

PUMPKIN HALVA

1.	Pumpkin	3 cups cooked, mashed
2.	Cake Flour	1 cup
3.	Honey	2 cups
4.	Butter	1 cup
5.	Cardamom Powder	1 ½ tsp
6.	Milk	1 ½ cup
7.	Almond & Cashews	½ cup chopped
8.	Vanilla extract	2 tsp

PREPARATION:

Peel, remove seeds and cut pumpkin into small pieces. Wash and drain. Cover and cook for 15 minutes till soft. Mash it well. Place in a non-sticking pot along with 1 ½ cups of honey and bring to a boil. Stir constantly. In a separate bowl mix flour with 1 ½ cups of milk and pour through a colander into the thickened pumpkin. Stir well. Add ½ cup of butter to prevent the mixture sticking to the bottom. As the butter is being absorbed put in the remaining butter and honey. Sprinkle in cardamom powder and chopped nuts. Add vanilla. Reduce heat. Check the doneness and when it is not sticky, turn into a greased tray and level the surface.

BLACK HALVA

1. Cake Flour   1 ½ cups
2. Coconut Milk   2 cups
3. Jaggery   1 cup
4. Brown Sugar   1 cup
5. Ghee (Melted Butter)   1 cup
6. Cashews   ¼ cup chopped
7. Cardamom Powder   ½ tsp
8. Nutmeg Powder   ½ tsp

PREPARATION:

Make a fine paste of cake flour, milk, and jaggery. Add brown sugar. Cook over high heat stirring constantly. When it boils reduce heat to medium. Do not allow it to stick on the bottom. When it thickens add ¼ cup of ghee. As the mixture gets thicker, add the remaining butter a little at a time. Add honey. When it is almost ready sprinkle in the spices and nuts. Take a little and check if a ball can be formed easily. If it does not stick, remove from heat. Turn into a greased tray. Level the surface.

RICE HALVA

Instead of cake flour use rice flour. Do the rest as in black halva.

DESSERTS

DESSERTS

CAKES & COOKIES

PERFECT CAKE

A basic recipe for many types of cakes

1. Cake Flour	2 cups
2. Eggs	5 large
3. Butter	1 ½ cups
4. Super fine Sugar	1 ½ cups
5. Milk	½ cup
6. Baking Powder	2 tsp
7. Vanilla Extract	1 tsp
8. Nuts & Raisins	½ cup
9. Caraway Seeds	½ tsp (optional)
10. Salt	½ tsp

PREPARATION:

Measure and sift twice flour with baking powder. Mix sugar and butter till light and fluffy. Separate yolk from white. Add the yolks and beat well. Beat egg whites stiff but not dry. Fold in ¼ cup flour at a time. Add egg white and milk alternately. Do not over mix. Add vanilla extract and caraway seeds. Grease and flour a rectangle tray. Pour in the mixture and bake at 350^0 F for 35 to 40 minutes.

DESSERTS

JAGGERY CAKE

It has a unique flavour

1. Jaggery	1 cup
2. Butter	1 ¼ cups
3. Cake Flour	1 ¾ cups
4. Baking Powder	2 tsp
5. Raisins	2 cups
6. Glaced Ginger	¼ cup thinly chopped
7. Eggs	5 large
8. All Spice	1 tsp
9. Orange & Lemon Rind	1 tsp each chopped
10. Salt	½ tsp

PREPARATION:

Soften jaggery by boiling in ½ cup water. When cool beat with butter till light and fluffy. Add chopped ginger, orange, and lemon rind. Add eggs one at a time beating thoroughly. Sift flour with baking powder and spices. Fold in the raisins. Gently fold in. Pour in greased and floured cake tin and bake at 350^0 F for 30-40 minutes.

Extra Recipe

DESSERTS

CARAMEL CAKE

1. Cake Flour — 2 cups
2. Butter — 1 ½ cups
3. Super fine Sugar — 1 ½ cups
4. Sugar — ½ cup for caramel
5. Butter — 2 Tbs for caramel
6. Baking Powder — 2 tsp
7. Milk — ¼ cup
8. Eggs — 6 large
9. Vanilla Extract — 1 tsp
10. Pineapple Extract — ½ tsp

PREPARATION:

Heat 3 Tbs water along with ½ cup sugar. Within 5 minutes sugar will melt and turn to dark brown. Turn off heat and add 2 Tbs butter. Stir constantly. Pour 3 Tbs warm water when the syrup cools. Heat again till all lumps dissolve. Set aside. Sift flour with baking powder. Beat butter and sugar till light and fluffy. Add eggs one at a time beating well. Pour in the caramel and mix. Fold in flour and milk alternately. Add both extracts. Raisins and chopped nuts can be added. Pour into a greased, floured tray and bake at 350^0 F for 35-40 minutes. Take a tooth pick and prick the centre. If it comes out clean, cake is ready.

DESSERTS

SPICY WHEAT FLOUR CAKE

1. Whole Wheat Flour — 1 ¼ cup
2. Baking Powder — 1 tsp
3. Eggs — 4
4. Ghee — 1 cup
5. Super fine Sugar — 1 ¼ cups
6. Butter — 2 Tbs
7. Cloves Powder — ¼ tsp
8. Cinnamon Powder — ¼ tsp
9. Nutmeg Powder — ½ tsp
10. Raisins — ½ cup
11. Cashews — ½ cup broken
12. Vanilla Extract — 1 tsp
13. Salt — ½ tsp

PREPARATION:

Sift flour and baking powder. Melt butter till it turns yellow and bubbles up. Before it turns brown remove from heat. This is ghee. Mix ghee with ¾ cup castor sugar till light and fluffy. Add salt. Separate the yolk and white of the eggs. Beat in the egg yolks one at a time. Keep raisins in boiled water ahead of time for at least 2 hours. Drain and roll in 2 Tbs flour. Make a caramel with ½ cup sugar and 2 Tbs butter. Cool and pour in. Add flour and egg white alternately. Add spices. Drop in raisins. Add vanilla extract. Pour into a greased and floured tray and bake at 350^0 F for 30 to 40 minutes.

DESSERTS

EASY COCOA CAKE

1. Cake Flour — 1 ¾ cups
2. Sugar — 1 ½ cup
3. Ghee — ½ cup
4. Yogurt — 1 cup
5. Eggs — 5
6. Baking Soda — 1 ¼ tsp
7. Cocoa Powder — ¼ cup
8. Vanilla Extract — 1 ½ tsp
9. Salt — ½ tsp

PREPARATION:

Mix sugar and ghee. Sift flour with baking soda. Add eggs one at a time and beat well. In ¼ cup water mix the cocoa to a fine paste and beat into the batter. Add yogurt. Pour extract and gently fold in the flour. Pour into a greased and floured baking tray and bake at 350° F for 30 to 35 minutes.

It is a moist rich cake.

DESSERTS

FOUR EGGS CAKE

Excellent for icing.

1. Cake Flour	1 ¾ cups
2. Baking Powder	3 tsp
3. Eggs	4 large
5. Sugar	1 ½ cups
6. Vegetable Oil	½ cup
7. Milk	1 cup
8. Banana Extract	1 tsp
9. Salt	¾ tsp

PREPARATION:

Separate white and yolk of eggs. Sift flour with baking powder and salt. Keep the flour in a big bowl. Make a well in the middle and pour oil. Add egg yolks, milk, and extract. Gently form a smooth batter. Beat the egg whites till stiff or standing on peaks. Fold this gently little by little into the batter. Do not over mix. When all meringue is added the mixture will be double in quantity. Pour into a greased and floured round tray and bake at 350^0 F for 30 to 35 minutes.

For beating egg whites stiff a little cream of tartar or vinegar will help. Measure ingredients accurately.

DESSERTS

NO EGG CAKE

1. Cake Flour   2 cups
2. Honey   ¾ cup
3. Oil   ½ cup
4. Yogurt   1 cup
5. Cocoa   2 Tbs
6. Baking Soda   1 ½ tsp
7. Baking Powder   ½ tsp
8. Vanilla Extract   1 tsp
9. Chopped Nuts   ¼ cup
10. Raisins   ¼ cup

PREPARATION:

Sift flour, cocoa, baking powder, and baking soda. Soften honey. Add yogurt. Beat together. Add oil and flour alternately. Soak raisins in boiled water for 1 hour ahead of time, drain and roll in a little flour. Add chopped nuts and raisins. Add vanilla. Turn it into a greased tray and bake at 350^0 F for 30 to 35 minutes.

DESSERTS

CARROT APPLE CAKE

1. Carrots & Apples — 2 cups grated
2. Cake Flour — 2 cups
3. Brown Sugar — 1 ½ cups
4. Fruits — 2 cups
   (Dates, banana, raisins)
5. Oil — 1 ½ cups
6. Eggs — 3
7. Baking Soda — 1 ½ tsp
8. Cinnamon Powder — 1 ½ tsp
9. Cloves Powder — 1 tsp
10. Salt — 1 tsp

PREPARATION:

Sift flour with cinnamon, cloves, baking soda, and salt. Mix grated carrots, apples, sugar, and fruits. Add egg yolks. Stir with a spatula. Add oil. Fold in flour. Beat egg whites and fold in. Pour into a greased, floured baking tray and bake at 350^0 F for 35-40 minutes or till done.

DATES CAKE

1. Cake Flour — 3 cups
2. Super fine Sugar — 2 cups
3. Dates — 1 cup chopped
4. Eggs — 5
5. Water — 1 cup
6. Baking Soda — 1 tsp
7. Baking Powder — ½ tsp
8. Ghee — 1 cup
9. Vanilla Extract — 1 tsp
10. Salt — ½ tsp

PREPARATION:

Soak chopped dates in warm water and baking soda for 2 hours. Cream ghee and super fine sugar till fluffy. Add egg yolks and continue beating. Add dates and water. Mix. Sift flour with baking powder. Add to the mixture along with beaten egg whites. Add extract. Turn into a greased tray and bake at 350^0 F for 35 to 40 minutes.

DESSERTS

FRUIT CAKE

1. Cake Flour — 2 cups
2. Mixed Fruits — 4 cups
3. Cashews — 1 cup chopped
4. Raisins — 1 cup
5. Butter — 1 ½ cups
6. Sugar — 2 cups
7. Baking Powder — 2 tsp
8. Eggs — 6 large
9. Ginger Glazed — ¼ cup chopped
10. Brandy — 1 Tbs
11. Vanilla Extract — 1 tsp
12. Cinnamon Powder — ¾ tsp
13. Cloves — ¾ tsp
14. Nutmeg — ¾ tsp
15. Salt — ½ tsp

PREPARATION:

Make caramel with ½ cup sugar and 2 Tbs water. As it turns brown remove from heat and add 1 Tbs butter. When cool add ¼ cup water. Heat to break all lumps. Set aside. Beat sugar and butter till fluffy. Add eggs one at a time and beat well. Sift flour with baking powder, salt, and spices. Pour in caramel. Combine. Add all chopped fruits and raisins with the flour and gently fold in. Pour in brandy and vanilla. Mix and pour into greased floured tray and bake for 1-1 ½ hour or till done.

This cake will be more delicious upon sitting a day or two.

DESSERTS

DESSERTS

NANKATAI

1. All Purpose Flour — 2 cups
2. Butter — ¾ cup
3. Sugar — 1 cup
4. Cardamom Powder — 1 tsp
5. Cherries — ¼ cup (red & green)
6. Baking Powder — ½ tsp
7. Baking Soda — ½ tsp
   Salt — ½ tsp

PREPARATION:

Cream butter and sugar. Add flour, salt, and cardamom powder. Blend well. Make small balls, and flatten top. Place a cherry on top of each and bake at 350^0 F for 15-20 minutes.

DESSERTS

GINGER BISCUITS

1. White Flour   2 cups
2. Dried Ginger Powder   2 tsp
3. Cinnamon Powder   1 tsp
4. Cloves Powder   1 tsp
5. Baking Soda   1 tsp
6. Molasses   ½ cup
7. Sugar   ½ cup
8. Egg   1
9. Ghee (Melted Butter) ½ cup
10. Salt   ½ tsp

PREPARATION:

Sift flour with spices and baking soda. Mix melted butter, molasses and sugar together. Add flour and beaten egg. Knead and make small balls. Flatten and bake at 350⁰ F for 15 to 20 minutes.

DESSERTS

COOKIES

OATMEAL COOKIES

1. Oatmeal (quick)	2 cups
2. White Flour	2 cups
3. Baking Powder	2 tsp
4. Butter	¾ cup
5. Honey	½ cup
6. Sugar	½ cup
7. Egg	2
8. Milk	2 Tbs
9. Vanilla Extract	1 tsp
Salt	½ tsp

PREPARATION:

Mix melted butter, honey, sugar, and egg yolk. Add vanilla extract and milk along with the flour mixed with baking powder and salt. Add oatmeal. Beat egg white till stiff and add. Knead well. Form into balls flatten and bake at 350^0 F for 15 to 20 minutes.

Extra Recipe:

DESSERTS

PEANUT COOKIES

1. Peanuts — 2 cups broken
2. White Flour — 2 cups
3. Castor Sugar — 1 ½ cups
4. Melted butter — ¾ cup
5. Egg — 1
6. Cloves Powder — ½ tsp
7. Cinnamon Powder — ½ tsp
8. Cardamom Powder — ½ tsp
9. Baking Powder — 1 ½ tsp
   Salt — ½ tsp

PREPARATION:

Sift flour with baking powder and salt. Cream butter and sugar. Add flour along with peanuts. Add beaten egg and spices. Make a smooth dough. Roll into any desirable shape and bake at 350^0 F for 15-20 minutes.

DESSERTS

QUICK APPLE PIE

1.	Apple	2 cups (sliced thin)
2.	Sugar	1 cup
3.	Ghee	¼ cup (Melted Butter)
4.	Buttermilk	2 Tbs
5.	White Flour	1 cup
6.	Eggs	2 (medium)
7.	Salt	¼ tsp
8.	Cinnamon powder	½ tsp
9.	Nutmeg Powder	¼ tsp
10.	Broken Cashews	¼ cup (optional)

PREPARATION:

Mix white flour, salt, and ghee. Add ½ cup sugar. Pour well beaten eggs and butter milk. Mix thoroughly. Place sliced apples in a greased pie dish and sprinkle ½ cup sugar, nutmeg, and cinnamon. Drop the batter evenly over the apples. Spread 1 Tbs sugar and cashews on top and bake at 350^0 for 35 - 40 minutes or till golden brown. Serve hot or cold.

SWEET DISHES (PAYASAM)

VERMICELLI DESSERT

A wonderful dessert! Give a try.

1. Vermicelli   2 cups
2. Tapioca   2 Tbs
3. Butter   2 Tbs
4. Sugar   1 ½ cups
5. Milk   5 cups
6. Water   2 cups
7. Cream   ½ cup
8. Cashew Nuts   ½ cup broken
9. Raisins   ½ cup
10. Cardamom Powder   1 tsp
    Salt   ½ tsp

PREPARATION:

Break vermicelli to 2" long pieces. Heat 2 Tbs butter and sauté vermicelli in low heat for 3 minutes and set aside. (Roasted vermicelli can be bought) Stir fry raisins and cashew nuts in 2 Tbs butter over medium heat for 1-2 minutes and set aside. In a heavy bottomed pot bring to a boil 2 cups of water and add tapioca. Stir and simmer for 3 minutes. Pour 3 cups of milk and allow to boil. Stir in vermicelli. Season with salt. When vermicelli becomes soft, add sugar. Pour in the remaining milk. Melt 2 Tbs butter till golden yellow and pour into the boiling mixture. As it thickens

DESSERTS

add raisins and cashews. Mix cardamom powder in some milk and pour in. Lastly add cream, allow to boil and remove from heat. Serve hot or cold.

DESSERTS

CREAM OF WHEAT DESSERT

1. Cream of Wheat   ½ cup
2. Milk   6 cups
3. Butter   5 Tbs
4. Water   1 cup
5. Cardamom Powder   ½ tsp
6. Cashews   ¼ cup broken
7. Raisins   ¼ cup
8. Sugar   ¾ cup

PREPARATION:

Fry cream of wheat in 2 Tbs butter till crisp (for 1-2 minutes). Fry cashews and raisins in 1 Tbs butter till golden brown and set aside. Boil 1 cup water and 5 cups milk together. Add cream of wheat. Stir constantly to avoid sticking. As it thickens add sugar. Pour in the remaining milk. Melt 2 Tbs butter till golden yellow and pour into the boiling mixture. Add raisins and cashews. Sprinklele cardamom powder. Combine. Bring to a boil. Serve hot or cold.

DESSERTS

RICE DESSERT

1. White Rice — ½ cup
2. Milk — 5 cups
3. Sugar — 1 cup
4. Ghee — 2 Tbs (Melted Butter)
5. Cardamom Powder — ½ tsp
6. Coconut — ¼ cup sliced thin
7. Cashews, Raisins — ¼ cup each

PREPARATION:

Boil 1 cup of water and 2 cups of milk together. Add rice. Stir occasionally. Meanwhile in another pot fry coconuts till golden brown. Fry cashews and raisins in butter till golden brown and set aside. When rice is almost cooked add sugar and ghee. (Melt butter till it turns golden yellow. i.e. ghee). Stir and cook for 2 minutes. Add the remaining milk. Allow to simmer for 3 minutes. Add fried coconuts, cashews, and raisins. Mix cardamom powder in some milk and pour in. Stir well. Bring to a boil. Serve hot.

DESSERTS

MUNG BEANS DESSERT

1. Mung Beans	½ cup
2. White Rice	¼ cup
3. Jaggery	1 cup (Brown Sugar)
4. Ghee	¼ cup (Melted Butter)
5. Coconut	¼ cup sliced thinly
6. Cashews, Raisins	¼ cup each
7. Cumin Powder	¼ tsp
8. Dry Ginger Powder	½ tsp
9. Cardamom	½ tsp
10. Milk	5 cups

PREPARATION:

Fry mung beans for 3-4 minutes till most of them change colour or they become crisp. Cook in 2 cups of water till soft. Boil 1 cup of water and add rice. When rice is half cooked pour 3 cups of milk. Add cooked mung beans. Bring to a boil. Add brown sugar and ghee. Stir for 5 minutes. By this time rice and green grams will be fully cooked. Add remaining milk, spices, nuts, and raisins. Bring to a boil. Serve hot or cold.

Split mung beans can also be used to make this dessert. In that case cook rice and mung beans together.

DESSERTS

ADA PRATHAMAN

1. Ada   1 cup
2. Ghee   4 Tbs
3. Jaggery   1 cup
4. Milk   5 cups
5. Cream   ½ cup
6. Cardamom Powder   ½ tsp
7. Dried Ginger Powder   ½ tsp
8. Cumin Powder   ½ tsp
   Salt   ½ tsp

PREPARATION:

Boil 3 cups of milk. Add 1 cup ada into the boiling milk. Stir continuously. After 2 minutes add jaggery. Cook ada over medium heat. Add 3 Tbs ghee. Simmer. Pour in remaining milk. When the mixture is thickened add all spices dissolved in some milk. Fry raisins and cashews in 1 Tbs ghee and add in. Pour cream, allow to boil and serve hot or cold.

Ada can be bought from oriental stores. If it is too thick boil 1 cup milk and add. Stir well and use.

★ ★

DESSERTS

FRUIT SALAD

1. Apple/Strawberry   ½ cup
2. Pineapple   ½ cup
3. Mango & Blueberries 1 cup
4. Grapes (seedless)   1 cup
5. Banana   ½ cup
6. Vanilla Essence   1 tsp
7. Sugar   ¾ cup
8. Cardamom   ½
9. Cloves Powder   ¼ tsp
10. Lemon Juice   2 tsp
11. Whipping cream   2 cups
12. Icing Sugar   1 Tbs

PREPARATION:

Cut and cube all fruits. Boil 1 ½ cups of water and sugar together. Add lemon juice, cloves, and cardamom powder. When cool add all fruits. Chill. Beat whipping cream with icing sugar and vanilla till stiff. Serve fruit salad topped with whipped cream.

Thanks
to all who are using
this book.

You may contact me at
Lizymatt1@gmail.com
for any questions or comments.

All the monetary benefits from this book are going to support an orphanage.

Feel free to buy and distribute the book as a gift and participate in helping the poor and needy.

www.ingramcontent.com/pod-product-compliance
Lightning Source LLC
Chambersburg PA
CBHW041431300426
44116CB00001B/1